The Eco-friendly House

Green is Beautiful

The Eco-friendly House

Green
is Beautiful

Published in Australia in 2009 by
The Images Publishing Group Pty Ltd
ABN 89 059 734 431
6 Bastow Place, Mulgrave, Victoria 3170, Australia
Tel: +61 3 9561 5544 Fax: +61 3 9561 4860
books@imagespublishing.com
www.imagespublishing.com

National Library of Australia Cataloguing-in-Publication entry:

Author:	Santini, Claudio.
Title:	Green is beautiful / Claudio Santini, Dafna Zilafro.
ISBN:	9781864703252 (hbk.)
Subjects:	Architecture, Domestic—Pictorial works.
	Ecological houses—Pictorial works.
	Sustainable architecture.
Other Authors/Contributors:	Zilafro, Dafna.
Dewey Number:	728

Edited by Beth Browne

Digital production by the Graphic Image Studio, Pty Ltd, Australia
www.tgis.com.au

Pre-publishing services by Universal Colour Scanning Ltd., Hong Kong
Printed on 150 gsm matt art by Paramount Printing Company Limited, Hong Kong

Contents

Acknowledgments

We have a saying in Italian, *Grazie al Cielo*, meaning "Thanks to the Sky"—for those things that have graciously arrived in our life, a gift from above. I could not have assembled such a glorious collection of images without the profound talent of the many architects in this book. Thanks also to my friend and partner in this endeavor, Dafna Zilafro, who assembled my scattered thoughts into a coherent story. Her words lift complex concepts off the page with refreshing clarity, igniting the imagination. Special thanks to Janamarie, my wife, whose partnership, encouragement and unconditional devoted support throughout this process have enabled me to fully explore my curiosity and passion. Together we have shared the joy and discovery associated with living in a green home, and together our eyes have been opened to its many treasures. I'm grateful to the dear friends who participated and contributed with kind words of encouragement and precious suggestions, derived from professional expertise and personal knowledge: Cristina Noé, Paola and Alessandro Gatti, Alain Gayot, and Andrew Bergman. I express my admiration and gratitude for Paul Latham, Alessina Brooks and their wonderful staff, the publishers who believed in the idea, and together with Dafna and myself shared a sense of enthusiasm and adventure about the project. I deeply respect their insights and their unrelenting pursuit of well-designed contemporary architecture around the world. Finally, thanks to my mother to whom I dedicate this volume with profound love and respect.

Introduction

A large, mobile solar panel on the roof, following the sun on its daily journey from east to west, immediately captured my attention. I didn't know much about renewable energy and sustainability at the time; however, as an architectural photographer, I had been curious about the early stages of the green movement. It had become a growing fantasy for me to live in one such energy-efficient home and so on that fateful day in 1997 when my wife and I entered a large metal volume on Greene Avenue, listed as "the ecological house," something told me that my life was about to change. We responded emotionally not only to the idea of the house, but also to the experience that it had to offer—generous light and space delighted our senses and calmed our minds. We purchased the home, and thus began my personal awakening to the wonder and beauty of well-designed, green architecture.

I was intrigued by the idea of living in a place that was thoughtfully designed to save energy. The choice—that is, selecting a green home over a traditionally designed home—was one that gave me a sense of lightness and clarity. It was at once engaging and interesting to participate in a new process of reusing, saving, and recycling. I now realize that our choice in that brief moment was one that would continue to bear positive fruit

on the world around us, and I am forever changed by the power of that realization. The house has become a tool by which I have discovered, step by step, a new way of seeing my day-to-day effect on the planet, and the impact that certain technologies, like solar power, could have on the world if applied on a large scale.

Since that time, we have learned to manage and understand the finer details of our house. We have adapted our lifestyle to the big open space that at first we shied away from. Our low-energy appliances save water and electricity, and the massive batteries in our garage accumulate power from the sun daily. The low hum of the system's inverter is music to our ears, and we watch with pleasure when the instrument indicates our house is completely self-sufficient. At times, we are even able to sell energy back to the grid, turning our electric meter backward.

Our home's designer utilized a combination of modern technology and centuries-old sustainable design principles to create one of the first technologically evolved green homes in America. Inside, however, we discovered a beauty that surpassed its energy-saving features. We relished the light pouring through the oversized window in our living room; the white, empty space that made us feel as if we were floating in candid

immensity. Our house was simply beautiful both in form and function—and wonderful to live in. I soon began to seek out this type of dual beauty in my daily work as an architectural photographer, and my resulting journey is documented on the pages of this book. I have assembled this diverse collection to show the beauty of green architecture in its many forms. Mid-century modernists demonstrated a good understanding of this duality in the way that they oriented homes on a site and utilized fundamentals of daylight, passive shading, and composition. The beauty of an ecological home may be manifested in the elegant way that sunlight kisses an interior floor, and in the way the same floor returns warmth to the home later that evening; it may be manifested in the rigorous shape of recycled elements, dually supporting the home's structure and expressed visually and texturally within the interiors. Capturing the integration between form and function in photography amplifies the formal balance, and calls us to dream of a beautiful, silent, abstract, sustainable environment. My hope is that this book will redefine the notion that "green architecture" is merely technical—to give vision, through my lens, into a world where sustainability is a building block of true beauty, inside and out. Enjoy the tour.

Claudio Santini

CHAPTER 1

Brighten Up:
Daylighting

Daylighting, hallmarking much of the world's most celebrated architecture, provides natural light to see, work, and play, and where desirable, can connect intimately the interior of a home with its surroundings. Well-executed daylighting creates stunning, appropriately lit spaces while saving energy. Energy savings include those resulting directly from utilizing less artificial lighting, as well as indirectly from reduced artificial cooling requirements, since electric lights produce tremendous heat when compared to natural lighting.

The daylighting process is an integrated one—a dance between art and science, architecture and engineering. A designer must understand factors like climate, geographical region, building orientation, luminance levels, contrast ratios, window-to-wall ratios, ceiling-to-skylight area percentages, and reduction in glare.

Effectively daylit walls consist of approximately 25–40 percent windows. While this percentage is not all that different from non-daylit buildings, the strategic placement of windows and skylights in relation to the sun and other influential site conditions makes the difference between a well daylit home and one that misses the opportunity to utilize the sun's generous rays.

Successful daylighting introduces as much controlled daylight as possible deep into the home's interior. The human eye can adjust to high levels of luminance as long as it is evenly distributed. In general, indirect light reflected off a light-colored surface will provide better lighting quality than direct sunlight. Clerestories—a small row of windows near the top of a wall—can draw light high into a room, producing a natural glow on the ceiling that mimics our experience of the sky. Skylights offer even deeper light penetration

while reducing the likelihood of excessive brightness. Also, sloping a ceiling away from the fenestration area helps increase the surface brightness of the ceiling further into a space. Different strategies play with clear and translucent glazing, low-E glass, and other coatings to achieve varying lighting effects in different places.

Different solar effects in different parts of the home can guide circulation, emphasize discrete areas, and create more effective spaces for work and play. Variety simulates what occurs in nature, and creates happy, vibrant spaces—humans thrive in naturally lit environments! Studies and common sense show that proper daylighting improves the overall mood and productivity of a building's inhabitants. Reduced lighting costs and the associated reduced cooling costs are simply icing on the cake.

Ferro Residence

Santa Monica, California
Architect: Enclosures Architects

Located in a suburban Santa Monica neighborhood, a single-story, 1650-square-foot wood-framed residence built in the late 1940s required major updates to remain useful to its owners. Natural daylighting, welcomed through new perforations in the space, transforms a once-darkened series of hallways and closed rooms into a bright, open atrium with volumetric interest and connection.

The new design removes low ceilings and exposed timbers to add vertical volume and openness to the main living areas. Skylights perforate a formerly enclosed dining room, now exposed to living and kitchen areas and forming the new central atrium of the main floor. The room bonds program areas one to another, flooding them with new special interest, light, spirit, and vitality. The variety of forms, colors, materials, light, shadow, and reflection originating from this new core animate and reorient the experience of the home.

A new galley kitchen with generous 30-inch-wide black granite countertops, pullout cabinetry, and energy-saving appliances and materials rejuvenate the cooking and entertaining experience. In the living room, a fireplace refaced with cherry wood and black granite materially mirrors kitchen elements, visually connecting the two rooms.

The architect carves out a new children's loft space within the cutout of raised ceilings, a mezzanine volume that projects above the dining room. From the loft, two windows look down onto the kitchen and dining room, unifying upper and lower volumes. An operable skylight in the loft controls temperature and light in the space without the need for artificial control.

1   Indirect sunlight filters through skylights to illuminate the central core of the living space

The home's adjusted entry sequence makes room for a new guest bedroom and bathroom, and a new 850-square-foot addition reframes the backyard and integrates it as usable space into the overall site plan. French doors provide access to the new outdoor barbeque to the north, while identical doors on the adjacent wall open to the new patio and rear yard.

Without abandoning the wood-sided gable features of the existing house, the new 27th Street elevation suggests a slightly more contemporary approach within context—and its interior is a whole new experience of light and space.

2   Skylights mimic the ceiling's playful geometries and bounce natural light throughout the kitchen area

3   The architect opened up the walls between living spaces, allowing light to penetrate deep into the home

4   Layers of color and light add interest to circulation areas

5   Crisp rays of sunlight decorate the dining room wall

2

3

"The variety of forms, colors, materials, light, shadow, and reflection originating from this new core animate and reorient the experience of the home."

4

5

Hatch Residence

Santa Monica, California
Original architect: Thornton Abell
Remodel by: Ignacio Fernando & Joyce Butler

Part of a multi-generational arts colony high in the Santa Monica canyons, the Hatch Residence provides the creative canvas for an artistic lifestyle that is intimate with the outdoors. The home's three original structures include the main house, a separate studio, and detached garage. In a glorious remodel that preserves the original tradition and style of the home, the architect replaced the original studio with a structure that contains a new garage and second-story guest quarters and converted the original garage into a studio for the new owners, also artists. The main house is reconfigured to make room for the new owners' larger family, all the while preserving the footprint and spirit of the original home.

The original house, built in two phases, follows the spirit of the early Case Study movement—openness, exposed structural elements, and a fluid relationship with the outdoors dominate the aesthetic. Interior walls terminate at 7 feet, the roof floating several feet higher atop a continuous series of clerestory windows.

On its southwest elevation, the home's generous glazing draws in natural light year-round, permeating the space across the abbreviated interior walls. Additional modest openings on the north side allow the home to breathe and cross-ventilate. A new stair volume features a large, mullion-less corner window and links the lower level to the second-floor master bedroom and bath. The stair tower contains operable windows at the top, drawing hot air up and out of the house in warmer summer months, rendering artificial air conditioning unnecessary. Transom windows above interior doors encourage further liberal air circulation between rooms. A sophisticated, barrel-roofed skylight with photo sensors draws daylight directly into the center of the house.

Concrete floors warm the feet through a restored hydronic radiant heating system. The system also permeates the upstairs floors, clad in responsibly harvested machiche hardwood. Concrete on the interior seamlessly connects with exterior walkways, expanding the home's spatial experience and rapport with the outdoors.

1   A generous terrace off the master bedroom faces west to capture the afternoon sun

"On its southwest elevation, the home's generous glazing draws in natural light year-round, permeating the space across the abbreviated interior walls."

3

2   Shortened interior walls allow light to pass freely between rooms

3   A long, arched gallery with high clerestory windows provides an unusual source of light to the main living space

4

4   Large windows above a concrete block wall provide ample daylight to the living room

5   Sunlight is filtered through landscaping into master bedroom windows

6   Master bathroom draws light through high clerestory windows

5

6

Chattanooga Townhouses

San Francisco, California
Architect: Zack | deVito Architects

Set in the upscale, family-friendly Noe Valley neighborhood of San Francisco, the Chattanooga Townhouses invite an inordinate amount of daylight into two wonderfully modern living spaces. Challenged by a typical 26-by-11-foot San Francisco lot, the architects relentlessly pursued a program of side-by-side units with equal access to daylight, ventilation, views, and outdoor spaces.

Organizationally, a center-dividing wall angled from front to back creates trapezoidal spaces, one end wide, one narrow. Clear, yet dynamic floor plans emerge from the angle and a dramatic stair divides the entire volume on both sides, creating playful changes in elevation with some rooms taller than others. Although unique, plans are clean, rational, organized, and functional.

The Chattanooga Townhouses absorb generous daylight through oversized front and rear windows and French doors. Retractable shades gently deflect unwanted heat gain in the summertime. In colder months, the homes' bamboo, fly-ash concrete, and low-toxicity wool-carpeted floors are heated through a radiant hydronic heating system.

Sunlight enters the space through a large skylight directly over the master stair. Rays penetrate deep into the three-story townhouses via a spectacular series of translucent acrylic stair pads, bouncing off light-colored walls along the way.

1 A soft glow illuminates the living room, even on one of San Francisco's many overcast days

The building's scale and massing hints at, rather than copies, the surrounding architecture from various periods with decidedly modern articulation. Familiar materials are expressed with contemporary flair. The form is clearly of its time, whilst utilizing familiar neighborhood elements such as bay windows and front garages with decks above. Corten steel planters soften the exterior façade, lending subtle warmth and color variation. Chattanooga's warm daylighting and delectable palette of renewable bamboo, fly-ash concrete, natural woods, and recyclable metals present an urbanite's eco-modern dream home—or two.

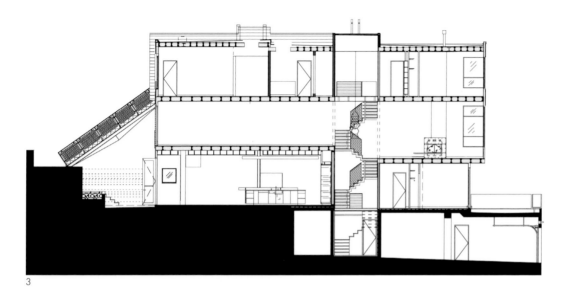

3

4

5

2 Corten steel planters add subtle color variation to a modern grey palette

3 A section illustrates the depth of the townhouses. Natural light is provided through windows in the front, in the back, and down the central core of the stairwell.

4 Constant backlighting from the stairwell illuminates the dining room by day

5 Daylight penetrates all three levels of the home through translucent acrylic stair pads

6

"Rays penetrate deep into the three-story townhouses via a spectacular series of translucent acrylic stair pads, bouncing off light-colored walls along the way."

7

6 A daybed takes advantage of light through corner windows, balanced by roller shades

7 A skylight provides ample task lighting to the bathroom vanity

CHAPTER 2

Contain the Comfort:
Insulation

Insulation is the single most important component in residential energy conservation and the cost of installation is well worth the benefits. Hidden within walls and above ceilings, insulation keeps a home warmer in winter and cooler in summer, easing the load on powered heating and air-conditioning systems. Insulation can also absorb unwanted sounds, reducing the noise from appliances, audio equipment, conversation, the street outside, and other sources of sound transmitted through walls and floors.

As insulation saves energy it also significantly decreases the diffusion of harmful air pollutants into the atmosphere. In fact, insulating homes can reduce the amount of nitrous oxide and sulfur oxide released into the atmosphere each year.

Recycled-content insulation now dominates the market, providing non-toxic energy savings out of otherwise disposable materials. Even fiberglass insulation now contains more than 25 percent recycled glass and renewable resources such as sand are used in its fabrication. According to the (USA) Glass Packaging Institute, fiberglass insulation is actually the largest secondary market for recycled glass containers.

Cellulose insulation offers one attractive alternative to fiberglass. Manufactured from shredded recycled newspapers with boric acid (also used as a fire retardant in children's pajamas), cellulose insulation provides the same insulation value as fiberglass for the same thickness. Cellulose is blown into attic cavities and is typically made from shredded recycled newspaper.

Other non-toxic alternatives to fiberglass insulation include cotton insulation made from shredded denim textile scraps, cement-coated air bubbles, and CO_2-foamed urethane.

Recycled content insulation packs the greatest sustainable punch—pound for pound, it saves 12 times more energy than is required to produce it. In addition to its priceless energy savings, this "wonder material" reduces pollution and keeps homes quiet, temperate, and happy throughout the seasons.

Wine Country Residence

Sonoma, California
Architect: CCS Architecture

A modest pavilion nestled deep within 5 acres of walnut trees and landscape, the Wine Country Residence humbly occupies a patch of former farmland, just outside downtown Sonoma. Its signature element, the traced outline of a barn roof, embraces the home on one end, as if to recall the land's agrarian roots.

The home's barn-like shelter provides energy-saving utility, passively shading the home's southern windows and offering an extra layer of insulation from the hot summer sun. The structure also creates welcome shade in some of the home's outdoor living spaces.

Underneath the aluminum superstructure resides the home itself—an unassuming, 20- by 100-foot box. The home's exterior walls and roof are uniquely constructed out of highly energy efficient Structured Insulated Panels (SIPs) rather than traditional stick construction. Prefabricated SIPs utilize less lumber and less energy to manufacture than traditional methods and at the same time provide superior insulation, allowing the home to retain its warmth in the winter and keep out unwanted heat in the summer. For texture, SIPs are clad with vertical slats of stained cedar over painted plywood, creating visual interest and an enchanting finished quality.

Within the walls of this gem, an open floor plan features two bedrooms, two bathrooms, and one large open space for cooking, eating, and living, equilaterally opened up to both sides of the site. A series of 8-foot-high sliding glass doors surround the perimeter of the home with light, views, and vivid connections to the land. Painted MDF cabinets complement bamboo floors, and flames dance from two gas fireplaces at opposite ends of the home. A latticed courtyard, swimming pool, and unbroken sightlines across the Sonoma Valley soothe the mind and spirit, entreating one to stay longer at this minimalist hideaway in the wine country.

1   A barn-like shelter provides a secondary layer of insulation from the hot sun

3

4

2 Walls constructed from Structured Insulated Panels (SIPs) provide superior insulation to typical wall sections

3 SIPs are clad with vertical slats of stained cedar for visual interest

4 A translucent corrugated overhang provides daylit shelter for an outdoor shower

5

"Prefabricated SIPs utilize less lumber and less energy to manufacture than traditional methods and at the same time provide superior insulation, allowing the home to retain its warmth in the winter and keep out unwanted heat in the summer."

5 A simple floorplan culminates at a central fireplace at one end of the home

6 A galley kitchen with sliding glass door provides natural light and views to the Sonoma landscape

7 Sunlight illuminates the home's main corridor

6

7

Piperno Residence

Siena, Italy
Architect: Luigi Villano

The Piperno Residence repurposes a former hay barn into a charming country cottage, its stone and brick walls emerging organically from the Chianti hillside. A structural palette of reclaimed fieldstones, timbers, and terra cotta roof tiles scavenged from other demolished cottages in the region add to the project's authenticity and low carbon footprint.

The architect utilizes a centuries-old technique to insulate the cottage from the humidity of the hillside. The technique involves a new wall, called a *scannafosso*, which creates separation and catalyzes ventilation in and around the home's exterior walls. In accordance with Italian tradition, the Piperno Residence utilizes its *scannafosso* to store wines, cheeses, and other foods that benefit from the aging process. At Piperno, the *scannafosso* also hosts components of the home's radiant heating system, which warms inhabitants through floors of sand-colored concrete and resin. Stone walls, 16 inches thick in places, naturally insulate the cottage, as well as provide thermal mass for passively heating and cooling the space.

The home is divided into two levels, the lower one containing bedrooms and the upper level housing the main living quarters. The living area consists of a three-sided volume with a central fireplace and walls covered in steel panels. Matching sand-colored window shutters accent large windows with low-profile frames. Facing southeast, the openings enjoy brilliant daylighting year-round and enviable views of the rolling hillside.

A rebuilt roof structure of reclaimed chestnut beams spans the main living space. The structure is supported by an oversized steel beam and an original stone column, which remains the main divider of the interior space. Lined with new bookshelves, the column loosely separates the dining room from an intimate conversation area.

Outside, the cottage's muted tones and irregular stone walls are one with the hill, an outcropping that appears born of the land itself. Sitting on a travertine bench—material salvaged from a home built in the 1600s—one is transported by the fragrant aromas of grasses, cypress trees, and wildflowers. In the summertime, the cottage disappears in an explosion of vegetation; in the winter, its stones blend with those scattered across the hillside, a reminder of the beautiful cycle of nature, death, and rebirth.

1 Walls of reclaimed field stones radiate with warmth in the evening

2

3

4

2 Reclaimed chestnut beams line and insulate the ceiling

3 Stone walls and concrete floors thermally insulate the home

4 A modern fireplace in the living room provides warmth in the heart of the home

5 A vertical window in the dining room reveals the thickness of Piperno's stone walls

6 A charming interior corner

7 A *scannafosso* insulates exterior walls from the humidity of the hillside

8 A corner stair with formed metal stair pads complements fieldstone walls

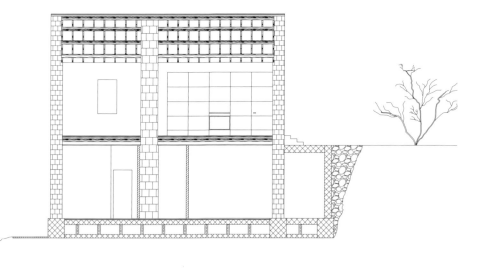
7

6

8

9

"The architect utilizes a centuries-old technique to insulate the cottage from the humidity of the hillside."

10

9   A vintage bed in the master bedroom

10   A modern sink rests on terrazzo countertops

Queen Anne Hill Residence

Seattle, Washington
Architects: David Coleman/Architecture

Sandwiched between craftsmen's homes on a sloped, urban lot in a trendy Seattle neighborhood, the Queen Anne Hill Residence provides an open, flexible floor plan in a modern cottage vernacular. Living areas occupy the main level, a master suite is located on the upper level, and children's rooms are on the lower level. Through the architect's careful positioning, an abundance of daylight and territorial views flood the home, and enclosed gardens and private patios dot its circumference with natural beauty.

The building is composed of four primary forms: a stuccoed "villa," two wood-clad sheds, and a terrace mediating between building and street. The terrace anchors the home visually to the site, and meets pedestrians with its stone entry stair. Containing the living room, the shed volume collides obliquely with the villa, injecting the room with a dynamic spatial quality and providing orientation toward the western sun and distant northern views. The shed's western wall penetrates the villa form, defining the entry and interior stairwells. Contiguous interior and exterior walls further erode distinctions between inside and out.

A loft-like quality permeates the home, which is intimately adorned with built-in cabinets, freestanding wardrobes, and playful wall fragments. A cabinet assembly between dining room and kitchen contains a built-in desk, shelves, a laundry, Swedish pantry, half bath and a fireplace. On the upper level, wardrobes on casters distinguish sleeping from dressing areas and allow for flexible room configurations. The home's lower level may easily be used as a separate apartment or incorporated into the main house, and its upper level is designed for conversion into an artist's studio.

The home shields inhabitants from Seattle's temperamental climate with extra-thick insulation—in some places exterior walls are up to 10 inches thick—and dual-paned, low-E argon-filled glass windows. An oversized cavity between the ceiling and gable-truss roof contains additional insulation material. Precious daylight and warmth are harvested through multiple windows and skylights in every room, and light-colored walls bounce the sun's rays throughout the house.

1 Exterior walls, in some places up to 10 inches thick, provide extra insulation

Wood floors are milled from 16-foot-long sheets of Medite®, a formaldehyde-free composite product made from postproduction waste. Other materials include birch plywood, quartzite, stucco, cedar siding and hard-trowel concrete. Low-flow water fixtures and low-energy appliances further reduce the home's carbon footprint.

As its modest bamboo orchard sways in the wind, the Queen Anne Hill Residence takes full advantage of nature's precious resources: harnessing the sun and protecting from the cold—an enviable urban oasis in one of America's great cities.

2 A shed volume collides obliquely with the villa

3 An overhang provides passive shading to the home's interior

2

3

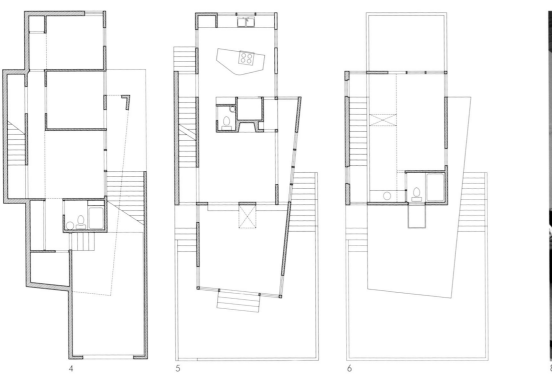

4 5 6 8

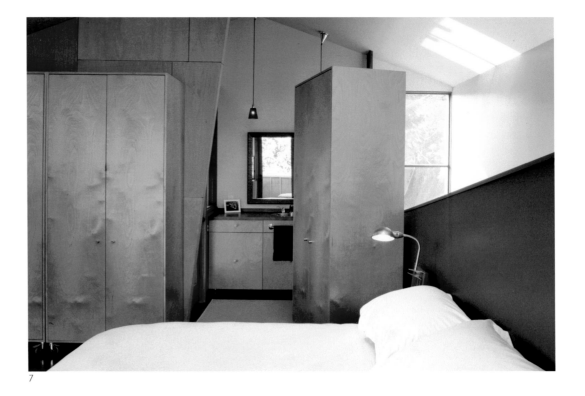

4–6 The building is composed of four primary forms that
      intersect on all three levels

  7 Custom cabinetry provides storage and division between
      rooms

  8 Light streams in through double French doors in the living
      room

  9 A cozy room enjoys warm insulation and natural light

7

"The home shields inhabitants from Seattle's temperamental climate with extra-thick insulation—in some places exterior walls are up to 10 inches thick—and dual-paned, low-E argon-filled glass windows."

CHAPTER 3

Adapt and Reuse:
Existing Buildings

Paralleling the phenomenon of recycling used products into newly formed products, the building industry has witnessed the increase of entire building recycling—arguably the greenest form of home design and construction. Whether adding to an existing home, converting an attic or garage, or reorienting an existing space for a new purpose, the decision to recycle an existing structure reduces urban sprawl, construction waste, and energy consumption.

The further a building's original purpose is from its new purpose, the more vision is required of the architect or designer in order to successfully convert the space. The real value in the existing building lies in the sheer volume of materials that are already on site and in place, which will not have to be purchased, shipped, and installed to create new structures. Successfully recycled homes creatively utilize the existing building and transform it into a new use in such a way that its history may be entirely indistinguishable from its final design.

"Adaptive Reuse" is the conversion of one type of building into another, such as a commercial warehouse into a residential loft space. More often than not, recycling a home simply means preserving structural materials and built elements from an original house and integrating those into a new format.

Materials from older buildings often possess an interesting or unique personality when incorporated into a new home. Reclaimed timber framing, thick tongue and groove wood floors, large steel roof trusses and exterior cladding of antique bricks and stone can become natural assets in the redevelopment of an existing structure, often expressed in the architecture for character and effect. Artistic vision can guide the integration of new materials with old, seamlessly weaving new geometries, textures, and colors into the new design. The greatest service one can make to our planet when creating a new home is to consider recycling an existing one, giving it new life for decades to come.

Zifkin Residence

Marina del Rey, California
Architect: Ted Tokio Tanaka, FAIA

Almost 20 years after its glorious birth in Marina Del Rey, a former duplex received its call to new life as a single detached home. The client had purchased both units on the property, and rather than tear down an architectural masterpiece, the Zifkins contacted the original architect to explore repurposing the building.

The original two units, on 8200 square feet of combined beachfront property, shared a structural bearing wall down the middle. In the final design, the wall is removed and replaced with a shaft of natural daylight penetrating deep into every corner of the building. Natural daylighting also penetrates the Zifkin Residence through skylights and myriad clerestory windows. From its various sources, daylight bounces across stark white walls, dancing and subtly changing hue from dawn until dusk. In the heat of summer, automated shading devices control the amount of direct sunlight and heat gain, assisted by the stunning natural breezes off the Pacific Ocean. As a result, electric lights and temperature controls are rarely necessary.

High ceilings and ample wall space showcase the clients' impressive art collection, and communal living spaces share a panoramic view of the Pacific Ocean, resembling a multilevel ocean liner. A formal living room faces the ocean on the ground level, an open kitchen, breakfast nook, and lounge area occupies the second level, and the master bedroom comprises the third level. Toward the back of the house, a garage and housekeeper's room occupy the ground level; a dining room with glass dome light shaft and two bedrooms make up the second level; and a mini-gym, library, bedroom, and study room comprise the third level, which is opened up via an oversized skylight and clerestory. The rooftop deck spanning the 40- by 90-foot parcel offers unbroken views of the ocean for entertaining, communing with family, or solitary meditation.

The simple palette consists of white walls inside and out; light-beige Italian sandstone flooring, fireplace surrounds, and hearth; lightly finished hardwood flooring; brilliant blue Brazilian granite countertops; and soft blue glass tile in the kitchen that subtly references nautical themes. Dramatic use of natural light, transparency, and reflection incorporate striped clear and frosted glass entrance doors, clear and frosted windows, a frosted glass countertop at the entrance hall, clear glass dome in the study above the dining room, and striped clear and frosted glass roof deck flooring over the master bedroom.

One floats effortlessly through the newly configured building—its smooth transitions elusive and convincing, a practical repurposing of timeless design.

1 A former duplex in Marina del Rey becomes a single family residence

2

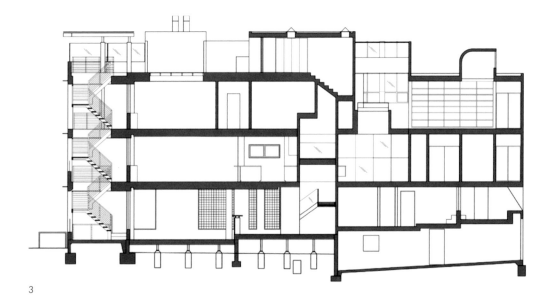

3

2 A glass dome allows light from third-story skylights to penetrate the lower floors of the home

3 The architect adapted the home's circulation to accommodate a single family

4 Wall colors subtly change throughout the day with the movement of the sun

5 A skylight floods the formal dining room with natural light

4

5

"One floats effortlessly through the newly configured building— its smooth transitions elusive and convincing, a practical repurposing of timeless design."

6 The central stair reflects the home's nautical theme

7 Master bedroom skylights are controlled with electronic shades

6

7

Hammett Residence

Los Gatos, California
Architect: Mark English Architects

"Adapt, reuse, and recycle," expresses the mantra of this unlikely, reborn Los Gatos tract home. A modest 1960s home, the dilapidated original required either complete destruction or thorough restoration. Client and architect responded with a creative and sustainable design solution, incorporating the client's penchant for and collection of vintage furnishings and materials.

The architect–client team conceived a mythology surrounding the house whereby its origins emerged from a historic agricultural compound. A central barn-like foundation and core becomes the design element around which the rest of the home's organization flows. One enters into the main pavilion to high ceilings and exposed, reclaimed old-growth timber framing—historic elements intimating the home's fictitious origins.

Beams, recovered from old barns across California, are nailed together with large sections of rebar hammered together with sledgehammers. Board and batten siding on the structure also derives from old barns. Old walnut siding, repurposed as flooring in the master bedroom,

lends authenticity and charm to the antiquated farmhouse. Reclaimed flagstone clads the entry and exterior walls, most likely salvaged from commercial building demolition.

Kitchen cabinets, fixtures and appliances reclaimed from old projects, and the client's large collection of vintage appliances, furnishings, and other pieces are incorporated into the final interior design. Colorful paints complete the aesthetic and complement the warm hue of old wood finishes.

The unlikely marriage of this 1960s structure with 100-year-old timbers and eclectic materials provides fodder for thought—sometimes the most responsible and beautiful design solutions emerge from re-envisioning elements for a new chapter in life.

1 The residence mimics a historic agricultural compound

3

2

2 The kitchen features reclaimed walnut floors, complemented
   by white country cabinets and tile countertops

3 An elevation of the home illustrates its façade variations

4 A warm hearth of recycled brick

5 Eclectic furnishings, reclaimed from various projects

4

5

6 A vintage chandelier lights a corner lounge

7 Flagstones, reclaimed from a commercial building project, clad one of the home's pavilions

8 Exposed timbers, reclaimed from old American barns, lend charm and character to the interiors

6

7

"Old walnut siding, repurposed as flooring in the master bedroom, lends authenticity and charm to the antiquated farmhouse."

Danny's Loft

Venice, California
Project by: Danny Kaplan

An addition to a 1924 warehouse, once home to the *Venice Vanguard* newspaper's printing press, Danny's lofts take advantage of the original building's high ceilings and open architecture. Two separate units, one 3000 square feet and the other 4000 square feet, occupy the renovated space, expressing much of the raw warehouse interior in the finished architecture.

Renewable bamboo flooring partially covers original concrete floors, and a tankless water heater provides energy-conserving hot water on demand. A tall shaft of light and space around the central stair draws air up and out of the house, providing generous natural ventilation and daylighting. A roof deck and multiple garden spaces provide connectivity with the outdoors. A freestanding fireplace, open on three sides, hints at separation between a media room, living room, and formal dining room, grounding the wide-open floor plan with warmth and hospitality.

From the street, the three-story addition hides behind the original building, appearing separate to passersby. The warehouse maintains its nondescript art deco façade and solid wall of glass block, re-envisioned in the 1940s. Past the carport, one enters the loft from a new garden space, around and through the 11-foot-tall, 5-foot-wide pivoting glass doors into the living room and kitchen. The home's largest volume—a three-story-high shaft of light surrounding the central stair—provides light to the kitchen, and stitches together the interiors from old and new construction. Teak cabinets with Corian countertops adorn the kitchen, which in turn provides entrance into the 1500 square feet of warehouse space housing the main living areas of the lofts. The new structure contains the main entry and kitchen/family room on the ground floor, with two upstairs bedroom–bathroom suites on the second and third floor, each with its own private terrace.

Meandering through the loft, old and new harmoniously collaborate to produce a living space that is at once open and intimate, contemporary and rich with history.

1   Loft interiors express roof trusses and HVAC equipment from the original warehouse building

2

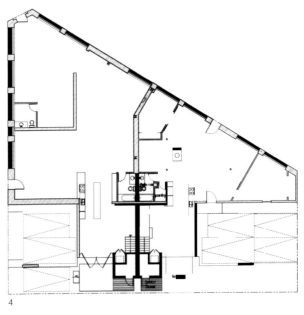

4

2 A new addition hides one façade of the original warehouse

3 A perforation in the brick walls frames views of bamboo landscaping

4 A floor plan shows compact living units created by the addition

"Meandering through the loft, old and new harmoniously collaborate to produce a living space that is at once open and intimate, contemporary and rich with history."

5 Glass block and clerestory windows filter light to a sitting room
6 A freestanding fireplace provides visual separation between functional areas of the living space
7 Custom cabinets and modern appliances upgrade the loft

5

6

7

CHAPTER 4

Filter the Sun:
Passive Shading

While the admission of sunlight and warmth during the day is absolutely paramount in green design, mitigating the sun's undesirable effects—over-brightness and unwanted heat gain—also contributes to a home's overarching energy conservation profile.

Passive shading keeps the direct sun off a home's glass in the summer and allows it to fall on the glass in winter. It considers the home's location and climate, keeping temperatures moderate and comfortable throughout the seasons.

Orienting a house with its longest walls facing north and south reduces exposure to intense morning and evening sun to the east and west. Properly designed roof overhangs can provide sufficient sun protection for south-facing glass, their length determined by the way the seasons interact with the specific site conditions. In the summer, when the sun is high in the sky, overhangs should be long enough to shade the interior completely. In winter, when the sun is lower, the same overhangs should allow the full sun to enter, warming the air, floor, walls, and other elements that have thermal mass.

A variety of passive shading techniques can mitigate the sun's rays on east- and west-facing glass; movable, opaque screens such as roller blinds or curtains are extremely effective, although they do impede view and air movement through the space. Adjustable or fixed louvers offer similar shading, but allow both air movement and views, and provide additional security where desirable. Trellises, trellised vines, shutters, and shading screens are other useful options.

Myriad glazing alternatives, including tints, fritting, metallic and low-emissivity coatings serve to reduce or eliminate heat gain through the glass. Multi-paned lites of glass are also readily available with inert-gas fills, such as argon or krypton, which further improve protection values.

Nature too provides a host of shading possibilities. Deciduous trees and vines, oriented outside south-facing windows filter the direct sun in the summer when leaves are full, then allow penetration in winter when leaves fall. Trees may

dually act as whole house overhangs, lowering internal temperatures by shading the roof and blocking direct solar gain. Creeping vines on the walls, green roofs, or extra layers of light-colored structure above the roof or around perimeter walls can additionally insulate walls from heat gain. Such extra layers provide an increased surface area for radiative emission and a cover of still air over the roof that impedes heat flow into the building, while still permitting upward heat flow at night.

With proper orientation, overhangs, strategically placed louvers, trellises, and vegetation, a home can stay cool during its hottest months without impeding daylight, airflow, and connection with the outdoors during the rest of the year. A cool place on a hot summer day, the well-shaded home is a refuge and joy throughout the seasons.

Kuperberg Residence

Beverly Hills, California
Architect: Sintesi Design

High up in a Beverly Hills canyon, the Kuperberg Residence cheerfully boasts interiors as green as its forested site. A few smart design interventions to the 1950s bungalow illuminate a new, ecological way of living in the house.

At the entrance, a tall canopy emphasizes transition from city to peaceful shelter. Operable skylights flood living and dining rooms with sunshine, each skylight mirrored by its equal-width, pivoting glass door below. Adjusting skylights, doors, and windows allows varying degrees of ventilation and natural temperature control without the use of forced air.

In the kitchen, a lacquered Masonite wood panel traverses the back wall, a canvas for naturally worn cherry cabinets and recycled copper pipes creatively fashioned into furnishings and fixtures.

The master suite is a single, open volume with an exposed vanity counter connecting sleeping and bathing areas. A freestanding, sculptural shower provides subtle separation between the two.

Accentuating outdoor living spaces, teak louvers passively shade patios and southern-exposed windows, complementing the Japanese-inspired landscaping. In the backyard, a teak patio, consisting of a deck-like base, a lounge seating area, and overhead trellis provides a transitional space between garden and interiors. Directly adjacent, a sunken, indoor/outdoor tub invites relaxation underneath a private skylight and slatted teak screen.

From the exterior, the Kuperberg Residence maintains a look very similar to its original 1950s design. On the inside, however, a transformed ecosystem utilizes nature's gifts to cool, brighten, and comfort the inhabitants. Sustainable bamboo floors, energy-saving appliances and low-voltage lighting minimize the home's eco footprint—in a town not necessarily known for conservation.

1 From the street, the home's 1950s appearance remains unchanged

2

2 Oversized doors pivot on center

3 A slatted screen shelters a private outdoor bath

4 A sunken tub enjoys filtered views of the Japanese-inspired garden

3

4

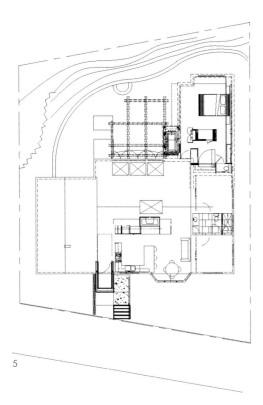

5

5 The addition seamlessly integrates with the original home

6 Oversized skylights align with pivoting patio doors

7 A transparent shower divides master bedroom and bathroom

8 An Eames Lounge Chair enjoys solace in the master bedroom

6

"Accentuating outdoor living spaces, teak louvers passively shade patios and southern-exposed windows, complementing the Japanese-inspired landscaping."

7

8

Shaw Residence

Los Gatos, California
Architect: Mark English Architects

Inspired in large part by Inca architecture wedged into unforgiving hillsides, the Shaw Residence marries intuitively to its site, preserving and celebrating the land's rugged natural beauty.

Nestled between a former orchard below and a hilltop condominium development above, the Shaw Residence occupies an unlikely suburban 2-acre parcel—a west-facing hillside anchored by a soothing creek below. Grassland, oak-covered California bay trees, and the beginning of a coastal mountain range collaborate to provide a winning canvas for responsible architecture.

The architect envisioned the house's organic form as a rock outcropping that had been exposed to its gentle, creekside amphitheater, tempering the elements through passive shading, strategic orientation, and cross-ventilation.

Its west-facing façade features a short wall with a long, extended roof overhang, passively shading the most sun-exposed façade. The overhang protects low, creekside windows, which draw breezes in and through the house during warm summer months. Elsewhere, high clerestory windows allow hot air to vent upward, establishing desirable cross-ventilation.

Upon entry, a "mud room" provides transitional space for removing shoes and unloading packages from the day's activities. Half a level down from the entry the lowest level of the home contains communal living and dining room spaces, adjacent to the creek and terraces. Here, the round dining room provides the home's stable and ceremonial center. Stepping up a half level from the entry, a full-fledged activity zone houses a graphic arts studio, homework room for the children, libraries, a wine cellar, and a small home theater. An upper story contains the bedrooms and more private areas of the home.

Hydronic radiant heat warms the house via thermal tubes underneath certified maple floorboards. By utilizing radiant heat rather than air to heat the home, thermal energy is retained even when windows are open. An energy-efficient tankless water heater feeds the radiant system, and zone-controlled thermostats in each room enable users to maximize the efficiency of the system, heating only rooms that are in use at any given moment.

1   The roof's generous overhang shields windows from direct sunlight during the most intense hours of the day

Structurally, the home utilizes sustainable, engineered timbers rather than old-growth lumber, lighting is low voltage, and recycled denim insulation lines the exterior walls and roof.

Visually undisturbed by its nearby suburban environment, the home's volumes hug the hillside, comfortably and ecologically adorned on the interior. Its gabled roof sequentially segments as the building curves in plan, and reduces in height as the footprint diminishes in width. The exterior is finished with natural copper sheathing at the façade and roof edges, wood siding, China Jade slate terrace paving, and recycled wood product Trex™ decking—materiality that playfully interacts with the eco-palette of the surrounding topography.

2 The sunken living room enjoys a warm fire
3 A massive vaulted ceiling with high clerestories draws filtered sunlight through the trees

"The architect envisioned the house's organic form as a rock outcropping that had been exposed to its gentle, creekside amphitheater, tempering the elements through passive shading, strategic orientation, and cross-ventilation."

3

4

5

4 A narrow stairwell illustrates the home's steep angles

5 A hanging mobile creates intimacy in the casual dining room

6 The home's profile clings tightly to the hillside

7 Formal dining room

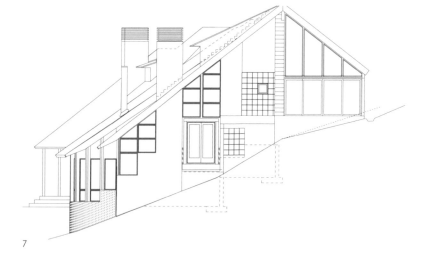

7

6

Skyline Residence

Hollywood, California
Architect: Belzberg Architects

Hovering on a ridgeline of the fantastic Hollywood Hills abutting beautiful conservancy land, the Skyline Residence represents an economical approach to creating an environmentally sensitive home with a minimal carbon footprint.

Principally, the design utilizes textbook passive shading techniques to control climate inside the house. A visually prominent folded plane, the roof overhangs the glass walls exactly enough to shelter the windows from direct sunlight in the summer. In the winter, the lower morning sun reaches underneath the overhang and floods the house with light and warmth that is absorbed by terrazzo and concrete floors. The floors radiate back warmth after the sun goes down—the simple design creates a passive heating condition in the winter and shading element in summer.

The roof plane folds solidly down the western elevation to face the late-afternoon setting sun, providing heat and glare protection during the region's hottest part of the day. At the bottom of the plane, a small window maintains visual connection with the landscape that penetrates the overhang toward the floor.

Facing south, an iconic screen of sustainable Xteri wood filters direct sun and wind into the home's main corridor through a wall of operable windows. The screen creates a visual dance of light on the interior and regulates the wind's movement into the house.

Recycled materials such as concrete with 15 percent fly-ash content and terrazzo floors with 50 percent recycled content are used throughout the home. Drought-tolerant plants and other landscaping elements, salvaged from other projects doomed to be demolished, make up the raw ingredients for Skyline's beautiful landscape. A saltwater pool eliminates typical pool chemicals in an environment where they would otherwise harm cherished wildlife.

To reduce carbon emissions from transporting materials, the architect and builder sourced almost all of the Skyline's construction materials from local yards, and recycled nearly all of the project's construction waste. In a low-budget project where high-tech systems such as photovoltaic panels, wind turbines, and recycled products are out of economical reach, the Skyline residence shows that purchasing locally, siting responsibly, and using basic passive shading and heating techniques to harvest and control the sun's precious energy can create the foundation for a happy, sustainable home.

1 An infinity pool overlooks the Los Angeles skyline

2

2 The folded metal roof plane passively shades south- and west-facing glass

3 The roof's intersection with the site creates interesting geometries and framed vistas

4 The north side of the home utilizes floor-to-ceiling glass to maximize natural lighting

5 Main entry

6 A section drawing illustrates the folded roof plane

7 A screen of louvers across translucent glazing passively shades the main corridor from direct sun

8 View from the interior through the entry door

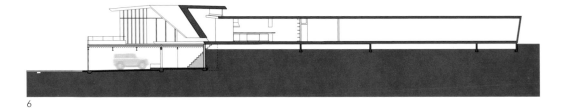

6

7

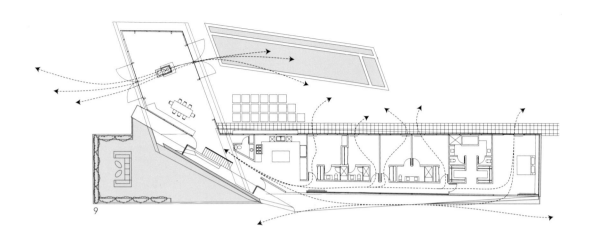

9

12

10

11

"A visually prominent folded plane, the roof overhangs the glass walls exactly enough to shelter the windows from direct sunlight in the summer."

9   Ventilation diagram
10   Floor-to-ceiling glass is sheltered slightly by roof overhangs
11   Giant doors offer ventilation control
12   Polished concrete floors reflect daylight into the home
13   Minimal furnishings abstract the interiors and emphasize transparency
14   An organic-shaped bathtub floats above the city

13

14

CHAPTER 5

Walk on Warmth:
Radiant Heating

Radiant heating consists of "radiant energy" emitted from a heat source; this radiant energy, or heat, penetrates all objects in its path, including people. The Romans are widely credited with introducing underfloor radiant heating, with a system called the "hypocaust." A slab floor was raised about 2 feet off the ground, supported by a series of tiled pillars, and walls were kept hollow. A "praefurnium," or wood-fired furnace below the floor emitted hot gasses that naturally flowed underneath the floors, up the walls, and out through the house, radiating heat along the way. Recent archeological evidence suggests that the practice of underfloor heating actually originated in South Asia some 5000 years BC.

Whoever invented radiant heating, there is no doubt that the efficiency and effectiveness of modern-day systems is contributing toward a resurgence of this most comfortable and energy efficient form of temperature control.

Hydronic (liquid) systems, the most popular and cost-effective radiant heating systems, pump heated water from a boiler through tubing laid in a pattern underneath the floor. In some systems, regulating the flow of hot water through each tubing loop controls the temperature in each room. The flow is regulated through a system of zoning valves or pumps and thermostats. Concrete, stone, or hardwood floors are the most common conductors of radiant heat.

More healthful than forced air, radiant heat systems do not blow dirt, dust, pollen, dander, or bacteria around the house. They are more efficient than baseboard heating and usually more efficient than forced-air heating because no energy is lost through ducts. Hydronic systems use little electricity, a benefit for homes off the power grid or in areas with high electricity prices, and a wide variety of energy sources may be used to heat the hydronic systems, including standard gas- or oil-fired boilers, wood-fired boilers, solar water heaters, or some combination of these heat sources.

Underfloor and wall heating systems often are called low-temperature systems, because the internal air temperature for radiant heated homes may be lower than for a conventionally heated home to achieve the same level of body comfort. Like standing in the sunshine, the sensation of comfort is caused by a combination of air temperature and radiant energy that equals the body's energy needs.

Manhattan Beach Residence

Manhattan Beach, California
Architect: LeanArch

At once subtle and radical, every detail of the three-story, three-bedroom Manhattan Beach Residence was designed with energy efficiency and long-term ecological concerns in mind. The home's beauty is testimony to the architect's ability to poetically weave ecological objectives into a comfortable, livable respite from the busy beach environment outside.

The small home's western elevation takes full advantage of its location across from the Pacific Ocean. Two large steel moment frames support 35 feet of floor-to-ceiling glass across the middle and top floor—the largest residential span of glass in the City of Manhattan Beach, and the most distinctive feature of the house. In another structural feat, the contrasting mass of the eastern wall rises, untouched by second- and third-story floor plates, as a 24-foot vertical channel of natural light and ventilation. A teak stairwell lines the wall, and as one climbs upward to the second and third floors, an exquisite visual drama unfolds. Thirty-five-foot windows and decks, playfully cantilevered to soften the modern design, span the entire west side of the home. The 180-degree view of the ocean includes large measures of beach, sky, water, and the Manhattan Beach pier.

Outdoor deck projections are seamless extensions of the floor plates, slivers that extend just beyond

the window wall. Fully extended, aluminum-clad north and south walls frame the decks and provide protection from the low summer sun, minimizing heat gain through the west-facing glass. Inside, electronic Mecho shades on an astrological timer diffuse light according to seasonal needs.

During summer months, small side vents inside the home open to allow rising hot air to exit, drawing cooler air up from the basement's concrete floor. During cooler months, the system works in reverse, assisted by concrete fiber panels lining the eastern wall interior. The panels absorb heat from the skylight above, and provide additional radiant heat throughout during cooler months. These panels were originally designed to line kiln ovens, to retain and distribute heat evenly.

A thermal heating system is embedded in the second and third floors and controlled via thermostat from independent zones in the house. The product conducts heat via aluminum sheeting underneath the home's second- and third-story hardwood floors more efficiently than through concrete, the material more commonly associated with radiant heating.

1   Radiant heat warms the home through rich, sustainable Cumaru flooring

A complete palette of sustainable materials complements structural considerations: Cumaru flooring—a fast-growing Brazilian teak that is environmentally certified for its sustainability—is used throughout the home's upper floors and finished with a water-based urethane. Dunn-Edwards Ecoshield paints, containing almost no petrochemical products and none of the toxic solvents found in most other paints, are used for interior walls. Appliances and lighting fixtures are energy efficient, the home's aluminum siding is made from 100 percent recycled material, and the insulation is made from recycled blue jeans. South and north-facing exteriors are clad in 100 percent recyclable corrugated aluminum panels made from 85 percent recycled content, and concrete fiber panels are also 100 percent recyclable. The integral colored, polished concrete floors require no sealers, and solar panels supply between 70 and 80 percent of the home's energy requirements. A port in the garage provides electricity for an electric car. Two tankless, or "on demand" hot-water heaters supply all of the home's hot-water needs—one for the residential plumbing functions and the other for servicing the radiant heating system.

Two rails, 16 feet apart, hang suspended solar panels like louvers above the roof. Invisible from below, externally the panels integrate subtly with the modern structure and framing of the home. Like all of the other sustainable features of the Manhattan Beach Residence, the panels are a subtle reminder that ecological priorities can be integrated quietly and poetically into a beautiful piece of architecture.

2 Extended north and south walls of recycled aluminum provide passive shading to west-facing terraces
3 High clerestory windows provide natural lighting and ventilation to bedrooms while maintaining privacy

2

3

4

"The home's beauty is testimony to the architect's ability to poetically weave ecological objectives into a comfortable, livable respite from the busy beach environment outside."

4   Recycled content wall and floor tiles line the master
    bathroom

5   100 percent recyclable concrete fiber panels

6   Floor-to-ceiling sliding glass doors open living space
    completely to the outdoors

7–9 Section drawings reveal an eastern wall untouched by
     second- and third-story floor plates, allowing vertical
     passage of air between floors

5

6

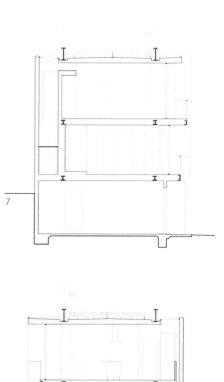

7

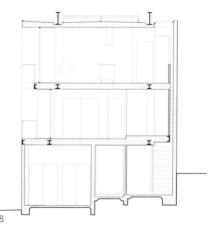

8

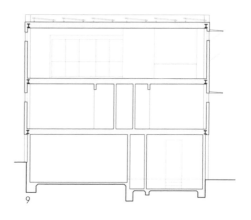

9

Strumwasser / Rahbar Residence

Thousand Oaks, CA
Original architect: A. Quincy Jones
Remodel by: Enclosures Architects

A merchant-builder in the 1950s, Joseph Eichler left his indelible mark on Southern California neighborhoods by creating vast enclaves of affordable, architecturally significant homes. Hiring some of California's notable mid-century architects, Eichler envisioned homes with modern amenities, simple floor plans, and ample room to enjoy the Southern California climate. With their dramatic façades, breezy interiors, soaring ceilings, and characteristic glass atriums, Eichlers are as relevant and desirable today as when they were first erected in post-war suburbs in the 1950s and 1960s.

Restoring and updating their A. Quincy Jones-designed Eichler, the owner/architects maintain the format and spirit of the house, while modernizing finishes and materials and making the home more eco-friendly. The couple restrains a minimal 250-square-foot addition underneath the home's generous, 4-foot cantilevered rooflines, taking advantage of A. Quincy Jones' original passive shading technique for cooling the interiors.

Eichler's signature central courtyard connects the living spaces intimately with the outdoors, giving visibility and transparency across program areas and drawing immense natural light and ventilation through the belly of the house. A restored radiant heating system under concrete floors efficiently warms the home in cooler months.

Solar panels on the south-facing pitch of the roof provide all of the energy necessary to heat the pool, and drought-tolerant plants amenable to Southern California's climate replace water-hungry grasses.

The entire Thousand Oaks development enjoys hundreds of mature trees, in spite of its urban setting. Houses are kept low to the ground, set back on lots and sheltered from direct view of the street, and all utility lines are run underground, virtually eliminating visual pollution.

Eichlers were among the first mass-produced homes in California to use many of the things that are now commonplace: sliding glass doors, built-in range and oven, metal cabinets, and radiant heat in floors. By the time of his death in 1974, Eichler had commissioned 11,000 distinctive homes throughout California. The Strumwasser / Rahbar Residence gently takes Eichler's vision one step further, updating, rethinking, and restoring a legend for the 21st century.

1   The Strumwasser / Rahbar residence from the street

"A restored radiant heating system under concrete floors efficiently warms the home in cooler months."

2

3

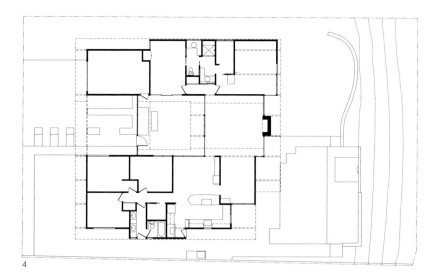

4

2 Louvers filter sunlight into a central courtyard

3 Courtyard draws light into the home's interior

4 Site plan

5 View from courtyard into living room

6 A comfortable study area offers natural light and cool breezes

5

6

Nordine Residence

Hermosa Beach, California
Project by: O plus L

A surfer's dream house, the Nordine Residence defies real estate trends in a busy Hermosa Beach market. On a parcel that many would have maximized with a 5000-square-foot building, the designer instead utilized the land to create the ultimate indoor–outdoor beach villa, a modest 2200-square-foot home.

The concept revolves around placing the smallest possible building on the site, adjacent to the largest possible outdoor "room." As a result, the home boasts one of only two swimming pools in the densely packed neighborhood, with a spa on its outdoor patio.

A mere 16 feet at its widest point, the L-shaped ground floor houses all of the public spaces and fronts the pool patio. The long leg of the L contains the home's main living spaces, and the short leg of the L contains the garage and upstairs office. Two 22-foot-long triple-track sliding doors disappear, unifying the ground floor completely with the outdoors. Consistent materiality across indoor and outdoor spaces blurs the separation further.

Throughout the interiors, a rich, expressed natural palette of wood, glass, and board-formed concrete accentuates differences: rough and smooth; hard

and soft; cut and molded. Ipe siding clads the exterior and terrazzo floors are heated through hydronic radiant heating.

Solar panels on the roof provide heating for the pool and the home's plumbing. Low-VOC paints, and off-site lacquering contribute to the home's healthy atmosphere as well as its ecological footprint. A basement room with 100 percent recycled carpet tile flooring houses the owner's extensive surfboard collection.

Prevailing breezes flow through the house from northwest to southeast—an operable skylight acts as a wind shaft to draw the air through the home when its sliding glass doors are open on the ground floor. As a result, no artificial air conditioning is necessary.

Multiple living rooms and spontaneous conversation settings dot the interiors, making the home feel larger than its 2200 square feet. A rooftop deck provides an extra enclave for reading, sharing a drink with friends or just watching the sunset on one of Hermosa Beach's many perfect summer nights.

1   Radiant heating warms the home through polished concrete flooring

2 A second-story
overhang provides
passive shading to the
first-floor pool area

3 Minimal decorative
finishes in the kitchen
and dining room

3

5

4   A board-formed concrete wall frames the fireplace and adds
    character to the living room

5   An iconic surfboard signals descent toward the owner's
    basement collection

6 A long custom sink and playful mosaic in the master bath, lit by high clerestory windows

7 Colorful textiles contrast smooth-troweled concrete in the master bedroom

8 The Nordine surfboard collection

9 Recycled carpet tiles line the stairs

6

7

"The concept revolves around placing the smallest possible building on the site, adjacent to the largest possible outdoor 'room.'"

8

9

CHAPTER 6

Renew and Reclaim:
Recycled Materials

Building and construction activities worldwide consume 3 billion tons of raw materials each year. Using recycled materials conserves dwindling, nonrenewable resources by reducing the amount of virgin material that is used in manufacturing processes. It also gives a new and often beautiful purpose to waste that already exists.

Most recycled building materials in use today consist of products fabricated from recycled or scrap materials, such as steel melted down from impounded automobiles or lumber that is engineered from scrap wood strands, veneers or other forms of wood fiber. In the case of engineered lumber, the finished product is actually stronger and more durable than the sum of its parts. Besides preserving precious forests, such wood generally does not shrink, warp, cup, crown, or twist. Cross-laminated plywood and oriented strand board, for example, distribute loads along the grain strength of wood in both panel axes. Glu-lam beams and wood I-joists can carry greater loads over longer spans than is possible with solid sawn wood of the same size.

Fly ash, a byproduct of coal burning plants, can provide similar strength and durability properties when recycled and mixed into concrete. Using concrete with fly ash content saves the material from a landfill destiny, and imparts desirable physical and chemical characteristics to the finished product. In addition to adding strength, fly ash also reduces permeability, reduces corrosion of reinforcing steel, increases sulphate resistance, and reduces alkali-aggregate reaction.

Materials found in a standard recycling bin—used bottles, paper, cans, and cardboard—form the raw materials for many recycled content products, in many cases contributing to their unique character and beauty. Recycled plastic melted together with wood chips forms stunningly practical lumber for outdoor decks. Insulation, such as fiberglass with some recycled glass, cotton made from recycled denim, or even newspaper recycled into cellulose insulation dually benefits a home's energy savings profile. Elegant ground coverings incorporate recycled glass chips into concrete or tile, and sustainable carpet tiles are fabricated from over

50 percent recycled plastic bottles. Numerous other inventive applications beautifully incorporate recycled content into countertops, floors, cabinets, and other interior and exterior finishes.

The most direct form of recycling is architectural salvage. In this exciting process, entire structural or design components from otherwise demolished homes, barns, and other structures are picked from the trash heap and are adapted to a new use in a new building. Such pieces often lend striking character and offer their new homes an instant sense of history and place.

Waste has a cost, which we all bear. The extraction, manufacture and transport, and disposal of virgin building materials clogs our landfills, pollutes air and water, depletes resources, and damages natural habitats. By mining this waste for valuable building materials, we contribute not only to the beauty of our homes, but to the ultimate preservation and beauty of our precious ecosystem.

Caner Residence

Located on a steep, west-facing slope of the Lovall Valley, the Caner Residence nestles into a saddle of land tucked behind a small knoll. Four individual structures allow the home to take advantage of the views and reinforce its intimate connection with the site. Vistas of the classic oak and grass landscape and of the spectacular views both west toward Sonoma and south toward San Francisco are framed.

The home's walls are constructed from Pneumatically Impacted Stabilized Earth (PISE)— a form of the oldest building method known to man. The thick, earthen walls provide thermal mass for the buildings, passive solar heating and cooling, and generally moderate temperature fluctuations. The natural earthen patina is complemented inside by an exposed roof structure of recycled fir trusses and salvaged cypress decking.

The complex consists of a carport building, guest quarters, main living and eating space, and bedroom wing. Exterior spaces link units as open-air hallways and grand outdoor living rooms, creating an expansive, campus-like sensation.

The three-story guest tower contains a ground-floor bedroom suite, an office on the middle level, and a covered deck at the top with sweeping views. During the afternoons, the tower casts welcome shade on the pool terrace. Deep loggias with rammed-earth columns shade the south- and west-facing rooms.

A recycled material palette includes roof trusses of reclaimed fir, ceiling decking of wood salvaged from pickle barrels, and a kitchen counter from part of a bowling lane—elements full of history and charm. Other countertops are made from recycled glass and scrap materials.

Wood siding, earthen walls, and metal roofing complement one another from inside out, where a patio of cast-earth pavers edges a modern lap pool and spa. At the main entry, an overhang protects a recycled Dutch door. The combination of materials and found objects hearkens to California's agrarian roots, synthesizing old world and native vernacular in a splendid retreat to mother earth.

1   A patio of cast-earth pavers lines a modern lap pool and spa

"Roof trusses of reclaimed fir, ceiling decking of wood salvaged from pickle barrels, and a kitchen counter from part of a bowling lane— elements full of history and charm."

2 A three-story guest tower contains a ground-floor bedroom suite, an office, and covered rooftop patio

3 A lazy hammock enjoys sweeping views of the property

2

4

4 Reclaimed wood trusses and siding create a warm interior palette

5 Ceiling fans and a covered patio provide a cool place to relax

6 Corner windows in the master bedroom

7 A window seat in the living room

Hybrid House

Culver City, California
Architect: Whitney Sanders Architects

Half prefabricated in warehouses and half built on-site, the Hybrid House stretches the imagination and delights the senses. A lightweight structural frame of recycled steel I-beams achieves an ingenious balance between ease of construction, responsible material use and the beauty of wide-open space.

Entering from the street, one briefly passes through a low entry corridor then emerges into the home's grand volume. Twenty-eight-foot ceilings accentuate the home's western façade—a wall collage of glass and translucent color panels that pour light and color onto concrete and bamboo floors, generating passive solar heat in cool months.

Musical architecture, so to speak, the colorful façade derives from a painting of a violin by Braque (*Aria of Bach*, 1913)—appropriate for the home's owner, a music critic.

The Hybrid House enjoys a flood of natural light, color and energy during the daytime. The large volume of the great room, combined with the slowly ascending stair and oversized landing create the perfect amphitheater for entertaining, meditation, or an occasional musical performance.

For this purpose, the shallow stairway features treads wide enough for two chairs each, leading to a suspended balcony. Transparent handrails allow unobstructed views across the space, accented by grasses laminated into the glass below eye level.

Above the landing, a whimsical spiral stair leads to a fort-like, sun-filled office for working at home. Sustainable, healthful materials are expressed throughout private and public spaces. One hundred percent natural Marmoleum® lines bathroom floors and shower enclosures. Low-VOC paints and eco-resin panels ensure no dangerous toxins enter the atmosphere.

At every turn, re-envisioned materials bring past lives to bear on the home, comfortable in their new surroundings. Adorning the master stair, rough-textured wallboards and built-in cabinets are fabricated from compressed sunflower seed hulls; shredded blue jeans take up residence in walls as insulation; recycled steel members form the structural framing.

1   A wall collage of glass and translucent color panels illuminates the western façade

The home recycles most of its gray water from showers, bathroom sinks, and other non-toilet uses to irrigate the garden and surrounding landscape. An on-demand water heater supplies both plumbing and a radiant heating system. Energy Star appliances, low-flow toilets and low-voltage task lighting further minimize the family's carbon footprint. The Hybrid House—part commercial warehouse, part single-family residence—comes together with surprising spaces and an earthy material palette; uncompromising beauty with a clear conscience.

2 The great room features double-high ceilings, lined with denim insulation. A spiral stairway leads from the second floor landing to a loft-like office space on the third floor.

3 Red laminate cabinets add a touch of color to an otherwise neutral palette

2

3

4

5

6

7

8

4 Bamboo-lined, wide, shallow stairs provide ample room for two chairs each during recitals. Built-in cabinets are constructed from sunflower seed hulls.

5 Spiral staircase

6 First floor plan

7 Second floor plan

8 Third floor plan

9

10

"At every turn, re-envisioned materials bring past lives to bear on the home, comfortable in their new surroundings."

11

9 Minimal seating in a small first-floor office

10 Daylight streams in through 3Form glass panels

11 Colorful, recycled content Marmoleum® lines all of the bathroom countertops in the home

12 A loft-like bedroom enjoys generous natural lighting

Sutton Residence

Novato, California
Architect: Sutton Suzuki Architects

Barns—the ones that the architect-owner remembers from growing up in rural Minnesota—inspired the design for the Sutton Residence in Northern California. The spacious floor plan and oversized openings reveal a fresh application to details once reserved for livestock and heavy equipment.

The house features a basic open organizational plan. Large barn doors, rather than the smaller hinged variety, slide on tracks to screen the office and bedroom for privacy. Huge sliding glass doors line the east side of the house, drawing in the morning sunshine. Large enough for a tractor to pass through, when the doors roll aside all hindrance is removed between the living area and the grandiose landscape.

Nature's resources, rather than artificial air controls, cool the house during the hotter months of the year. By its orientation toward the northeast, adjacent to the Petaluma River, the home avoids the intense southern and eastern sun. The property's three mature oaks passively shade windows during the heat of summer—in winter, they lose their leaves, allowing passage of the sun's warming rays.

Walking through the entryway, a single long room combines living, dining, and kitchen areas, with a cabinet providing vague separation between kitchen and dining room. A vertical shaft intersects one end, containing the master bedroom on one floor and children's bedrooms above, nestled like a tree house into the old growth canopy.

The beauty of the Sutton Residence lies in its clarity of plan and elemental expression of materials. Recycled beams from a 200-year-old Pennsylvania barn provide immediate depth and character, joists remain exposed and concrete unpolished. Radiant heat cycles through the floors, cool breezes enter through the barn doors, and the natural beauty of Petaluma's wildlife preserve moves through the heart of this unassuming home.

1   The Sutton Residence, amid its many old-growth trees

"Recycled beams from a 200-year-old Pennsylvania barn provide immediate depth and character, joists remain exposed and concrete unpolished."

2

3

2 The home's view of the Petaluma River
3 Recycled timbers from an old barn span the dining room
4 The home's wide perforations integrate interiors with the landscape and provide views from every room

4

5

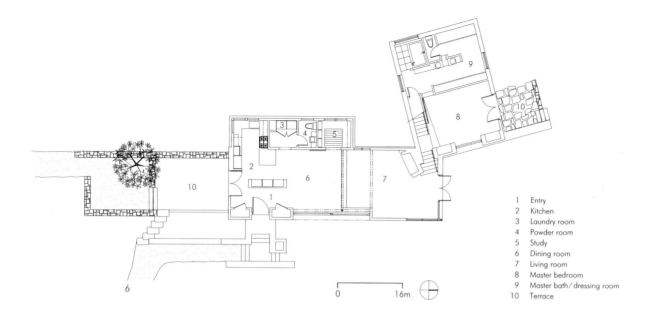

1	Entry
2	Kitchen
3	Laundry room
4	Powder room
5	Study
6	Dining room
7	Living room
8	Master bedroom
9	Master bath/dressing room
10	Terrace

5 A cozy master bedroom

6 Floor plan

7 A lounge takes in the endless view

8 Stairs from the children's room down to the main living space

CHAPTER 7

Tread Lightly:
Responsible Siting

Homes do not exist apart from their surroundings; rather they interact with the sites on which they are built. A green home is harmonious with the environment that it inhabits, preserving as much as possible of the existing vegetation, often minimizing the home's footprint to the smallest necessary area. In urban areas, a green home is also friendly to its neighbors, careful not to block important view corridors and to avoid unnecessary light and sound pollution to nearby homes.

Carrying out a careful site evaluation early can guide the design process, providing insight into the sun's movement across the land, soils, vegetation, and critical natural areas. Such information helps take advantage of a site's natural resources, while minimizing or eliminating any potentially negative impact on the surrounding ecosystem.

Clustering buildings or building attached units can preserve open space and wildlife habitats, avoiding especially sensitive areas like wetlands, and keeping roads and service lines short. Ideally, a home leaves the most pristine areas of its site untouched, and builds on areas that are less critical, or that may have been previously damaged. Removing invasive species of plants and downsizing high-maintenance turf areas, replacing them with diverse, climate-appropriate plants will further reduce the home's energy consumption profile.

Providing responsible on-site water management restores precious ecosystems by absorbing rainwater runoff back into the site, rather than carrying it off-site into storm sewers. Green roofs, or in arid areas, rooftop water-catchment systems, can collect rainwater and use it for landscape irrigation. Green building products, such as porous pavers further enhance the site's ability to absorb its own water runoff.

Finally, orienting the home to benefit both the landscape and the existing vegetation will make both homeowner and site happy for years to come. Trees on the east and west sides will naturally cool the home, and hedgerows and shrubbery can block cold winter winds or help channel cool summer breezes. Vegetation can mitigate automobile pollution and noise; landscaping and site design can provide seasonal shading, natural ventilation, daylighting, and a connection with nature that promotes mental and emotional health. Cumulatively, responsible siting has the potential to shape the public and ecological health of a neighborhood, region, and ultimately, the planet.

Treadwell Residence

Big Sur, California
Architect: Carver + Schicketanz Architects

On a rugged, 40-acre parcel overlooking the breathtaking Big Sur coastline, the Treadwell Residence modestly occupies 1900 square feet, minimally disturbing the natural ecology, and maximizing all that nature has to offer on its site.

Almost invisible to its nearest neighbors, the Treadwell Residence's most striking feature from the road is its undulating green roof of native grasses. The roof dually serves to insulate and to minimize the visual footprint of the home to its uphill neighbors. Utilities are routed underground, further minimizing the visual impact.

Three bedrooms and a great room with open kitchen face the astonishing, cliff-side western views. Bathrooms and other less-critical view areas occupy space underneath the green roof, carved into the hillside. A slight berm in the land shelters inhabitants from view of the nearby access road.

Sea breezes, natural ventilation, and passive solar energy permeate the home year-round. While most of the home's glass is oriented toward its western view, the architect carved an east-facing courtyard with full-height glass into the hillside. Sun streams through the glass in the morning to warm the stone floors, and during the coastline's many windy and cool days, the courtyard becomes a protected outdoor refuge for reading the paper or taking in the natural beauty of the mountainside. .

Natural interior finishes such as glass, wood, and stone blend with the existing colors of the native landscape. Limestone floors with hydronic radiant heating, low- to no-VOC paints, energy-efficient lighting design and natural wood ceilings contribute to a healthy, beautiful, and ecologically responsible lifestyle in the Big Sur wilderness.

1 The Treadwell Residence hugs the rugged Big Sur coastline

2

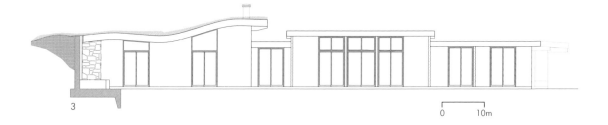

3

0   10m

2 An undulating green roof camouflages the house from
   higher on the hillside

3 The home's single-story elevation is simple and elegant

4 Breathtaking views from the cliffside spa

4

5

6

7

8

5 An all-glass southwestern façade makes the most of the home's stunning views to the ocean

6 An elevation drawing shows punctuations of wood siding and glass

7 An eastern courtyard steals the morning sun and looks through the house at dusk

8 Roof detail

9

"Almost invisible to its nearest neighbors, the Treadwell Residence's most striking feature from the road is its undulating green roof of native grasses."

11

10

9   Recycled timbers lend character to the fireplace column in the living room

10 Two modern lamps on a backdrop of varying wood details

11 Modern details nicely contrast with wood and glass

Brosmith Residence

Beverly Hills, California
Architect: Studio Pali Fekete architects (SPF:a)

The 4400-square-foot Brosmith Residence sensitively sites a single-family residence on a ridgeline of Mulholland Scenic Parkway, overlooking the San Fernando Valley of southern California. Like the minimalist beauties of the early California Case Study movement, the residence possesses an attractive simplicity and sensual use of commonly available materials.

Utilizing centuries-old best practices, the architect orients the residence to draw maximum natural light into the home, passively shaded by large roof overhangs. Courtyards with disappearing wall segments take advantage of the near-perfect California climate, alternatively welcoming sunshine and cool breezes according to which windows and doors are operating.

The house is organized along a central spine, broken into segmented living pods for different uses. Each "pod" is outfitted with its own version of an indoor–outdoor courtyard space, and each is connected independently to the central spine of the house. The architecture captures exterior space as living space within each of these courtyards. Pods include the master suite, the children's quarters, offices, caretaker's quarters, and public living space.

The common living space rambles at a slight grade down the hillside, from family room to kitchen, then dining room to formal living room. The entirety of the public space focuses inhabitants toward the floor-to-ceiling glass at the terminus of the living room, overlooking the infinity pool at the northern edge of the property. Furniture is kept low to the ground so as to keep views unobstructed, and the taller kitchen cabinetry suggests division between the home's public space and its central spine, without completely enclosing either.

Entering the common living areas, one is met with breathtaking vistas of the San Fernando Valley, which climax on the main patio where a glass-like swimming pool disappears entrancingly over the crisp clean horizon of the site's northern edge.

1 A teak-clad master bedroom gently occupies its hilltop site

1

The energy-conserving structure uses siting and natural shading from its orientation to reduce its dependence on mechanical environmental conditioning systems. Courtyard orientations take advantage of prevailing breezes. Innovative uses of standard materials create much of the custom feel of this residence, where concept and design elevate the feel of every room. A sliding louvered screen in the master bedroom uses an off-the-shelf, affordable aluminum frame fitted with aluminum louvers substituted for glass—a unique application that seamlessly integrates with the clean lines of the house. Readily available materials are fashioned resourcefully into architectural poetry.

2

"Utilizing centuries-old best practices, the architect orients the residence to draw maximum natural light into the home, passively shaded by large roof overhangs."

2 An infinity pool, tucked behind the landscape, enjoys sweeping views of the San Fernando Valley

3 The home's minimal volumes pause to allow outdoor circulation

4 View to the west from the patio

3

4

5

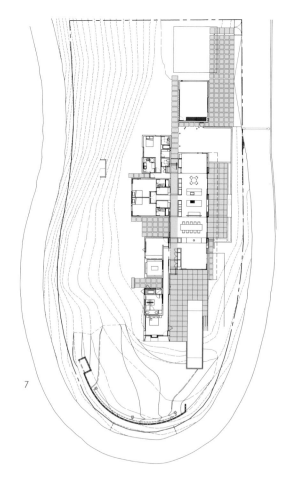

5   The living room is oriented toward the home's southwestern views

6   The main circulation corridor features high ceilings and clerestory windows that draw natural light in and through the home

7   A site plan shows the home's minimal footprint on the hillside

K-Ranch

Big Sur, California
Architect: Wormser & Associates Architects

Big Sur's land use authorities take preservation of its pristine environment seriously, and the region's strict guidelines set the tone for a stunning architectural solution at K-Ranch.

In order to minimize the visual impact of a large new single building, the architect spread out the home into three smaller structures on the 100-acre site, utilizing its outdoor transitions as part of the living experience. A main house, guesthouse, and playful barn/studio form the K-Ranch complex.

A palette of all natural materials celebrates the outdoors while capturing the spectacular views of Pfeiffer Ridge. A rough-sawn cedar frame and standing-seam copper roofs create a series of lofty spaces that are equally dramatic inside and out. Exposed framing provides a rich yet rustic character to the interior, and three sets of ocean-facing French doors in the main house unify the modest space under the canopy of eucalyptus with the rugged coastline and ocean views.

On the exterior, all three buildings feature beautiful red cedar shingles, teak doors, and red copper rooftops. Contemporary, handcrafted interior materials include custom-designed lighting fixtures and hand-wrought hardware, doorknobs and pulls with the owner's initial "K" hammered into their facings.

Complementing the main and guest houses, a small barn with a whimsically splayed gable roof plays host to an art studio for the children, equipment storage, and a materials workshop. The barn's two long walls slide open to create an open-air pavilion for musical performances, entertaining, or simply communing with nature.

Nestled on a ridge that gets early morning sun but is protected during the hot times of the day, the K-Ranch complex stays temperate and cool year round, delighting in the exquisite natural breezes climbing up the coastline.

1   The home consists of three distinct volumes woven together

2

3

"In order to minimize the visual impact of a large new single building, the architect spread out the home into three smaller structures on the 100-acre site, utilizing its outdoor transitions as part of the living experience."

4

5

2 The barn features a whimsically splayed gable roof

3 Children's bedroom

4 Barn interior

5 Old-growth trees support a hammock

CHAPTER 8

Feed the Grid:
Photovoltaics

What could be more beautiful than harnessing the boundless energy of the sun's direct rays to power a home's lights, appliances, and other energy requirements? The sun showers the earth every hour with enough energy to meet world demand for a year— energy that is pollution-free, inexhaustible, and directly accessible in most locations.

Photovoltaics (photo = light, voltaic = electricity), often referred to as solar energy, is a semiconductor-based technology that converts light energy directly into an electric current. The current may either be immediately used or stored, such as in a battery, for future use. Photovoltaics are usually made of silicon, the same material that makes up common beach sand, and cells are typically wafer-thin circles or rectangles, approximately 3 or 4 inches across. When photons in the sun's rays strike the surface of the silicon, they liberate electrons from the material's atoms.

Certain chemicals added to the material's composition help establish a path for the freed electrons, creating an electrical current. Through the photovoltaic effect, a typical 4-inch silicon solar cell produces about one watt of direct current electricity. For efficiency and practicality, multiple cells are wired together in a series and placed in glass-covered casings called modules, which in turn are strung together into larger arrays. Lightweight and versatile, these arrays can be easily mounted to rooftops, awnings, skylights, or built into the walls of buildings. New advancements in solar energy technology, such as solar shingles and transparent solar skylights add to the myriad ways that panels can be integrated into a home's design.

Photovoltaic cells come in three basic varieties: monocrystalline, polycrystalline, and amorphous. Monocrystalline cells are the most efficient but also the most expensive. They consist of a single crystal cut from an ingot of silicon. More common, polycrystalline cells are slightly less efficient, because they are made from silicone with several small crystals. Amorphous cells are made by spreading the silicon onto another material like stainless steel and, while cheaper to produce, they offer significantly less power than the other two types. The less power produced per panel, the more panels required to produce the same amount of electricity, hence the larger the surface area needed for installation. If space is not a concern, then less expensive amorphous cells may be the best option.

Expressed visibly from inside and outside the home, photovoltaics are often stunning design elements, casting prisms of light and reflection into a space. Their wafer-thin profiles, contrasted by plasma-like reflective skins, twinkle with timeless beauty like the sun.

Santini Residence

Mar Vista, California
Project by: John Picard

Built in 1990, a fledgling child of the green building movement, the Santini Residence is an incubator for timeless green principles and sustainable beauty. The two-story, galvanized metal box is cleanly articulated, a tasteful modern resident in its cozy West Los Angeles neighborhood. Steel, 70–95 percent fabricated from recycled automobiles and pre-cut at the manufacturer to minimize waste, forms the home's structural framing.

A rooftop array of moving solar panels track the sun's path throughout the day, optimizing their angle on its rays to absorb the maximum available energy. The home's extra insulation reduces the need for artificial temperature controls, and a light colored roof reflects ultraviolet rays, cooling the home naturally. Rooftop drains capture precious California rain runoff, channeling the water for use in the property's beds of drought-tolerant landscape. Sensors in the front lawn of slow-growing Bonsai dwarf grasses tell a drip irrigation system when there is natural rainwater present, shutting off the sprinklers when rendered unnecessary.

Sunlight pours into the oversized window in the home's great room, filtered passively by a preserved coral tree. Bamboo floors provide a renewable platform for scattered area rugs and furnishings

to loosely divide the space. Soaring white walls offer a generous canvas for artwork and occasional movie projection on one wall; a loft bedroom is tucked high under the open ceiling with exposed ductwork. A closet in the back bedroom drops a hidden ladder, leading up to a rooftop deck/meditation room.

From its foundation, the Santini Residence lives up to its Greene Avenue address—foundational concrete is formed with reclaimed rather than fresh water. Rebar in the concrete slab comes from melted-down reclaimed handguns from the Los Angeles Sheriff's office.

One of the first technologically evolved green homes in America, the Santini Residence highlights all that is beautiful about sustainable living at the household level. Its tasteful balance of technology and aesthetic gently leads the way, prodding with taste and civility toward a better future.

1 The Santini Residence from Greene Street

"A rooftop array of moving solar panels track the sun's path throughout the day, optimizing their angle on its rays to absorb the maximum available energy."

4

2 French doors open the living room up to the eastern sun

3 A translucent canopy filters sunlight onto the back patio

4 Clean lines and modern details in metal, glass, and wood

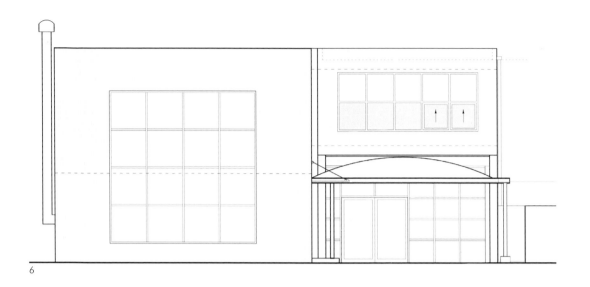

6

5

7

9

8

5 The Santini dining room

6 Eastern elevation drawing

7 An open kitchen

8 A wood stove warms the living room

9 An oversized living room window is divided into 16 quadrants

House Ocho

Carmel, California
Architect: Feldman Architecture

Sunken into the hillside, its rooftop covered in wildflower beds, grasses, strawberries, and succulents, House Ocho yields in form and material to the beauty of the surrounding Monterey Peninsula. Tall grasses and gnarled coastal oaks provide protection from wind and direct sun, and the home's living roof provides an added layer of insulation from temperatures outside.

The house sprawls from the hillside as three compact pavilions rather than one large structure, breaking up its overall massing, and enabling light to penetrate three sides of each pavilion. Spaces between pavilions become usable outdoor rooms, and a series of solar panels, integrated as panes of glass into skylights, form a visual spine, filtering direct sunlight into the submerged volumes of the home. The solar panels dually filter the light penetrating the night sky from inside the house, minimizing the impact of artificial light on the home's pristine surroundings.

Concrete floors, exposed, board-formed concrete walls, and large south-facing windows work together to facilitate passive solar heating throughout the house. For the windows that make up most of the southeastern walls, the architect selected a special glass that allows heat to penetrate while insulating the interior. A thermally retentive concrete retaining wall becomes the main circulation element in the house, providing heat to each pavilion in the winter and cool temperatures in the summer when windows are shaded during the day. Recycled denim provides insulation within exterior walls.

As fluid with the site as its native plant roof, House Ocho's materials palette—sandblasted concrete and exterior paint colors—precisely matches the deep gray and silvery green of the lichen-encrusted oak trees. Rusted steel used for the two chimneys matches the color of the bark on nearby manzanita trees. Exposed Douglas fir timbers reveal the layering and structure of the house, elementally tying it to the surrounding forest.

With its low profile, wide windows, and board-formed concrete walls, it is difficult to imagine a structure more at peace with its site than House Ocho, or more harmonious with the Santa Lucia Preserve.

1 House Ocho, nestled in its Santa Lucia Preserve site on the Monterey Peninsula

1

2

2 A photovoltaic array is visible from the interior of the home,
   where it filters sunlight through skylights

3 A thermal, board-formed concrete wall is visible from every
   room in the house

4 Exposed Douglas fir timbers in the mezzanine

3

"A series of solar panels, integrated as panes of glass into skylights, form a visual spine, filtering direct sunlight into the submerged volumes of the home."

5

5 A cozy fireplace and seating area

6 Corner windows in the guest bedroom reveal a lush Monterey landscape

7 A custom headboard offers both storage and visual separation

6

7

Scarpa Residence

Venice, California
Architect: Pugh + Scarpa

More air than building, the Scarpa Residence in Venice Beach outlines rather than encloses the life of a southern California family. Peering through its elegant, long strokes of horizontal and vertical lines one can see, from front to back, a house that epitomizes material innovation and a fresh approach to residential architecture.

The house is a dynamic composition of interlocking solids and voids; its visual corridors, stairs, bearing walls, structural columns, guardrails, built-in furniture, and cabinetry vary in density, color, and texture. Light permeates the interior of the residence at several locations, and a series of stepped roofs, glazed walls, and clerestory windows broadcast light from multiple directions.

Two slender, 25-foot-high, poured concrete towers frame the view 24 feet apart, capped by a thin, bluish canopy of solar panels, dangling playfully over one side. The striking array of photovoltaics provides most of the home's energy, shields the roof from direct sunlight, and provides passive shading to the second-floor terrace. When daylight kisses the panels, multicolored reflections dance across the home. Natural light and air permeate the living space from all sides, rendering artificial lights and temperature controls unnecessary

on most days. A fly-ash concrete base warms the house from the ground floor up through passive solar retention and a hydronic radiant heating system.

The home's main living volumes are loosely separated, and equally harmonious with an outdoor living space and pool patio. Upstairs, the master bedroom suite opens onto a deep covered patio overlooking the garden, an outdoor sleeping loft.

Outside, decomposed granite and permeable gravel allow the ground to absorb water and in turn mitigate urban run-off to the ocean. Integral colored pigment stucco on the exterior of the building eliminates the need for exterior paints.

Readily available recycled materials find non-conventional expression in the Scarpa Residence: Oriented Strand Board (OSB), a product of pressed-together recycled wood chips, is sanded and utilized for finished flooring and cabinet faces. Homosote, typically a sound-deadening under-carpet layment made from recycled newsprint, is sanded down to a suede-like texture and used as an interior wall finish.

1 Recycled materials find expression in the Scarpa Residence

"The striking array of photovoltaics provides most of the home's energy, shields the roof from direct sunlight, and provides passive shading to the second-floor terrace."

3

An exterior grouping of industrial broom brushes serves as a privacy screen for the upstairs patio. Perforated, recycled steel fabricates the staircase up to the master suite, casting pixels of light onto the floor below. As hot air rises, it passes through the staircase up and out of the house. Dividing the bath from dining room, a two-panel glass enclosure contains tiny plastic balls, ordinarily used to clean ocean oil spills. The home's unique palette of materials is expressed not only for structural honesty, as in the work of some modernists, but because of its raw, elemental beauty.

Whether the Scarpa Residence is a house or the built environment's version of a shelter tent, the home splendidly succeeds in the California climate, mocking unnecessary segregation between the indoors and the great, beautiful outdoors.

2

2 A photovoltaic array folds from the roof down one side of the residence

3 A concrete path crosses a Koi pond

4 Section drawing

5 A privacy screen is creatively constructed from industrial broom brushes

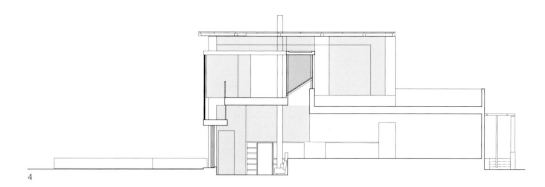

4

5

CHAPTER 9

Return the Heat:
Passive Solar

As bare feet bury themselves in warm sand on a cool spring day—or as a dog sprawls across a cool basement floor in the heat of the summer—passive solar heating and cooling techniques are organic and intuitive, as old as the earth itself.

Ancient Greeks and Romans used passive solar design and the sun to light and heat indoor spaces. Socrates wrote, "In houses that look toward the south, the sun penetrates the portico in winter." Romans advanced the art by covering south-facing building openings with glass or mica to hold in the heat of the winter sun. Through calculated use of the sun's energy, Greeks and Romans offset the need to burn wood that was often in short supply.

In passive solar heating, elements of the actual living space capture, absorb, and distribute heat from the sun. South-facing glass admits solar energy into the house where it strikes thermal mass materials such as masonry floors and walls. The thermal mass absorbs, and thus tempers the intensity of the heat during the day. At night, when outside temperatures drop and the interior space cools, the thermal mass radiates heat back into the living space. The re-radiation of collected daytime heat maintains comfortable temperatures during cool nights, and may continue to provide heat through several cloudy days.

In passive cooling, the system works in reverse. At night, thermal mass in the home absorbs and retains cool temperatures. If shaded from the sun during the daytime, thermal floors and walls remain cool, and emanate cool temperatures. Proper ventilation, fans, or other mechanical devices further the effect of either passive heating or cooling by circulating the air throughout the home.

Implementing passive solar techniques relies heavily on properly siting the home on the land. Designers will site passive solar houses on the portion of property that receives the most sunlight between the hours of 9:00 a.m. and 3:00 p.m. during winter months. Buildings generally oriented along an east–west axis are more efficient for both winter heating and summer cooling, allowing maximum solar glazing (windows) to the south to capture the sun's rays, and minimizing east–west exposure to the intense morning and afternoon summer sunlight.

A home's common areas—living rooms, dining rooms, family rooms, and kitchens benefit most from passive solar when located on the south face of the building. Alternatively, rooms least used, such as closets, storage areas, and garages are best located along the north wall where they can act as a buffer between high-use living space and the cold north side.

The passively heated home utilizes time-tested techniques, harnessing energy from the world's most available natural resource. Thermal masses of stone, natural earth, concrete, and other organic materials gently moderate the home's climate throughout the year, much as the earth itself adjusts to the seasons.

Sena Residence

Carmel Highlands, California
Architect: Carver + Schicketanz Architects

Located in the Carmel Highlands, a lush area of rugged beauty between Carmel and Big Sur on the northern California coastline, the Sena Residence incorporates a rich history into its newly fashioned habitat. Many of the home's finishes and interior materials come from reclaimed timbers and other recycled items. Once a table, the home's front door was purchased from the Anderle Gallery in nearby Carmel. According to the gallery owner, the table originated from the reclaimed wood floor of a 200-year-old temple in Korea that burned down. The home's plank ceiling stock is reclaimed from torn-down barns and fencing from around the Western United States. Wood trim on the interior and exterior posts, and the horizontal band above the windows and doors came from a salvaged, turn-of-the-century trestle bridge in St. Louis.

The Sena Residence takes glorious advantage of prevailing breezes and natural sunlight, in spite of its challenging north-facing site. Situated in a natural bowl, the home climbs a fairly steep slope and faces the ocean to the north with a window-filled façade and French doors. A sun-kissed patio carved into the hillside reaches for the southern sun, where most of the natural light and heat enter the home. French doors and operable windows draw both the sun and natural breezes in through this elevation. During cooler times of year, the southern uphill patio becomes a refuge from the harsher ocean climate, and draws necessary heat from the sun onto the stone floors. Passive solar heating, combined with high efficiency, hydronic radiant heat and low-voltage lighting minimize the home's artificial energy requirements.

Built for a family with children, the Sena Residence is as practical as it is beautiful, and as healthy as it is ecologically responsible. Oversized natural materials complement muted tones of low-VOC paints and nontoxic finishes. Elemental, not ornamental, the palette is durable, and the home's tremendous expanses of glass elevations frame aerial views of the peninsula meeting the Pacific Ocean.

1 The Sena Residence with its view of the Big Sur coastline in the background

1

2

2 Reclaimed wood on the front door derives from a 200-year-old Korean temple that burned down. The wood became a table before its new life as the Sena entry.

3 French doors on the eastern elevation draw morning sunlight into the home

4 Stone floors on a southern patio retain heat from the sun

"During cooler times of year, the southern uphill patio becomes a refuge from the harsher ocean climate, and draws necessary heat from the sun onto the home's stone floors."

5

6

5 French doors cast a decorative shadow

6 Daylight streams in through a high window

7 Elevation drawing

8 Master bedroom

9 Master bathroom

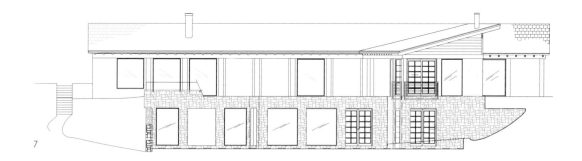

7

8

9

Warbler Way Residence

Hollywood, California
Architect: Robert Anderson, AIA

Striking on its treacherous canyon perch, the Warbler Way Residence takes full advantage of a Hollywood canyon's natural beauty, orientation, and near-perfect climate.

The backbone of this home's energy-saving strategy is also its most architecturally significant feature—a vertical central shaft that circulates passive thermal energy from the lower level's flamed limestone floors up through the second and third story of the home. A three-story span of windows acts as a skin for the entire volume to the south, and a series of mechanical shades dictates whether the ground floor will store warm or cool energy during the day, depending on the season. At nightfall, a sequence of mechanical fans joins forces with prevailing breezes to distribute stored energy up and around the home's various living areas.

Like many canyon homes, the Warbler Way Residence is humble and unassuming from the street. Upon entering the outer gate, one is greeted by a serene bronze fountain within a tiny courtyard, loosely covered with a white cast-iron lattice overhead. Walking through the front door, the view from Warbler's 45-degree hillside steals the show—a true Hollywood moment.

The home's street level contains parking for two cars, the entry, central stair, and an office that doubles as a bedroom. The center level houses the master and guest bedrooms, bathrooms, and closet spaces. The lower pool level grounds the home both thermally and socially, with its indoor–outdoor stretch of limestone floors leading from pool to living, dining, bar, and kitchen areas. At night, inhabitants ascend to privacy on the second story, effortlessly followed by a cool summer breeze.

1 A three-story span of windows draws sunlight into the home

1

2

Return the Heat: Passive Solar

"A three-story span of windows acts as a skin for the entire volume to the south, and a series of mechanical shades dictates whether the ground floor will store warm or cool energy during the day, depending on the season."

3

2   An infinity pool, overlooking the Los Angeles basin

3   The home's main entry

4

4 Limestone floors gather heat during the day
5 A service bar and dining table
6 The master bath enjoys sweeping views

5

6

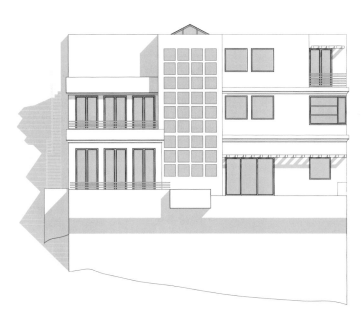

7

7 Elevation from the canyon

8 A three-story staircase provides the central circulation volume of the home

9 A daybed on the upper floor enjoys diffused sun from the skylight

8

9

Ashland Residence

Santa Monica, California
Architect: Michael W. Folonis Architects

The family had outgrown its 1950s post and beam home. Teenagers required their own rooms and their parents wanted a more private master suite and space to work in. Rather than tearing down an existing structure, the family preserved the home, adding an elegant, straightforwardly articulated addition and pool—room to work and play—while conserving precious natural resources. The architect's freestanding addition seamlessly integrates with the existing property and utilizes every inch of the original house in its redefinition of space and site.

The design generates new activity around a contemporary addition, pool, and landscaping. Both the home and its addition face a private, newly landscaped oasis and pool, creating multiple opportunities for indoor–outdoor living in the generous Southern California climate.

Bordering the pool to the northeast, the new volume features a master suite on the upper floor, a work studio on the ground floor, and a glass bridge connecting the two to the main house.

The ground floor studio, measuring only 10 feet wide by 35 feet long, opens poolside; its long glass wall is a series of disappearing sliders, creating the illusion of a much larger room. The second floor, cantilevered an extra 4 feet overhead enhances

the perceived width of the space, and provides passive shading from the sun during the hottest portion of the day. In winter months, the indoor–outdoor concrete floor acts as a heat sink, absorbing warmth during the day and distributing it to inhabitants during cool nights.

Occupying the top level of the structure, the master suite makes the most of its hillside ocean-facing view. Operable windows ventilate the room, taking advantage of prevailing ocean breezes, and an overhead trellis provides passive shading to the upper story during the day. Separate furnaces for upstairs and downstairs conserve energy and allow inhabitants to only heat or cool the portion of the space in use.

A student of the early Case Study maestros, the architect implements centuries-old techniques of daylighting, passive shading, and passive solar energy—increasing the lifetime and utility of a marvelously livable green home.

1 A new master suite passively shades an office below

2

"In winter months, the indoor–outdoor concrete floor acts as a heat sink, absorbing warmth during the day and distributing it to inhabitants during cool nights."

3

4

2　A columnless corner window in the new addition
3　New master bedroom with high clerestory windows
4　New master bathroom with colorful sink basins

5 A wide corridor enjoys various natural light sources
6 An elevation drawing shows the new addition
7 Art studio on the ground floor

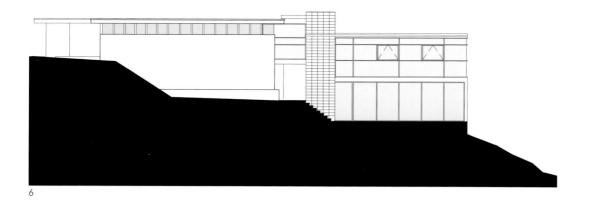

6

7

CHAPTER 10

Let it Breathe:
Ventilation

After the Second World War, the advent of central air conditioning—the sealed building—made natural ventilation an anachronism. Today, natural ventilation is making a comeback owing to rising energy costs and the worldwide movement toward green design. Architects and engineers are using advanced computer and modeling techniques to refine the physics of heating, cooling, and ventilating.

Ventilation is the intentional movement of air from outside a building to the inside—it is the "V" in "HVAC." Natural ventilation design provides ventilation to occupants using the least amount of resources possible, reducing or eliminating the need for energy-consumptive mechanical ventilation devices.

There are two basic types of natural ventilation occurring in buildings: wind-driven ventilation and stack ventilation. The majority of homes rely mostly on wind-driven ventilation, but the most efficient design for a natural ventilation building should implement both strategies.

Wind-driven ventilation, the oldest and most straightforward form of natural ventilation, admits cool night air to drive out the warm air of the day.

If breezes are predominant, high vents or open windows on the leeward side of a home (the side away from prevailing breezes) will allow the hottest air, located near the ceiling to escape, drawing cooler night air through low open vents or windows on the windward side. To maximize the cooling effect, leeward openings should have substantially larger total area than those on the windward side of the house.

Stack effect ventilation is temperature induced. When there is a temperature difference between two adjoining volumes of air the warmer air will have lower density and be more buoyant, thus will rise above the cold air creating an upward air stream. If breezes are minimal at the site, stack ventilation can still ventilate and cool the home, as long as the outdoor air is cooler than the indoor air at the peak of the house. The coolest air around a house is usually found on the north side, especially if this area is well shaded by trees or shrubs and has water features. Cool air intake vents are best located as low as possible on the north side. The greater the difference in temperature between outdoors and indoors,

and the greater the height difference between the low and high vents, the faster the flow of natural convection.

In an urban environment, drawing air through the house from courtyards avoids the direct pollution and noise of the street façade. Wind can augment the stack effect but also reduce its effect depending on its speed, direction, and the design of air inlets and outlets. Therefore prevailing winds should be considered before designing a stack effect ventilation strategy.

Natural wind-driven ventilation, augmented by the stack effect can create a continuous flow of fresh, cool air to indoor spaces, and remove unwanted odors, carbon dioxide, cooking and other emissions from the living space. As architects rediscover the benefits of fresh air ventilation as an alternative to hermetically sealed, air-conditioned buildings, they discover new architectural forms, reinventing residential architecture—using one of the oldest tricks in the book.

Harless Residence

Manhattan Beach, California
Architect: Dean Nota, AIA

Nestled on a tiny 30- by 52-foot parcel, the Harless Residence in Manhattan Beach illustrates the magnificent power of borrowed light and shared space. The architect utilizes a palette of materials and symbols familiar to the beach, from natural hued concrete block to the home's ship-like lanai, steel-framed and cantilevered from the southern façade.

The house is organized vertically on three levels, with the main entry, family room, and parking on the ground level, three private bedrooms in the middle, and a living room, dining room, and kitchen on the upper level. A stairwell, lined with translucent glass block filters light and silhouettes of dancing bamboo into the loosely structured core of the building.

From the modest entry up through the stairwell, the home reveals a succession of spaces that are progressively more open, dynamic, and ever increasing in light and view. Arriving at the top, one reaches the spatial highpoint of the building containing the main living and entertaining functions. Upper level wall planes tilt outward to the north and south as if to extend these spaces beyond the physical limits of the site.

The building's upper story steps aside its floor plan to harness precious daylight through bathroom skylights, one level below. Once drawn into the home's lower levels, light is shared throughout the building via a series of translucent glass walls; borrowed light enters the master bedroom and vanity, loosely separated by floor finish variations, but sharing space to afford each a larger experience.

Low-E glass coatings reflect the sun's hot infrared rays, and recycled metal panels on the roof and side walls further add to the cooling effect in California's hot summer months.

Taking advantage of the prevailing breezes of the south bay, the design incorporates basic passive energy techniques, utilizing natural ventilation to move thermal energy stored during the day in exposed concrete floors and concrete masonry walls. In the wintertime, unshaded skylights and windows allow the sun to heat the concrete mass—at night, a combination of mechanical fans and natural ventilation circulate the retained warmth up through the home. In the summer, the system works in reverse, shading windows during the daytime to keep the concrete mass cool and then circulating the cool air at night throughout the home.

1 Concrete block, aluminum panels and glass create a modern composition

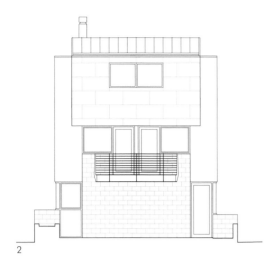

2

3

2 Elevation drawing

3 A series of shades control the admission of direct sunlight

4 A comfortable seat by the fire

5 An upper-level dining room

4

5

"Taking advantage of the prevailing breezes of the south bay, the design incorporates basic passive energy techniques, utilizing natural ventilation to move thermal energy stored during the day in exposed concrete floors and concrete masonry walls."

6 Heat circulates up through the home's main stair

7 A mechanical fan assists with ventilation in the master bedroom

6

7

Beuth Residence

Los Angeles, California
Architect: Studio Pali Fekete architects (SPF:a)

Perched on a steep, nearly 45-degree grade, the Beuth Residence is a four-level, multifaceted viewing station for the Los Angeles Basin below. Teak panels clad the upper level of the house, seemingly floating on air, above an all-glass main level. Jutting off the master bedroom, a Miesian sitting room steals 180-degree views of the Los Angeles Basin stretching from the Getty Museum to the skyscrapers of downtown LA. The residence is grounded by a crisp concrete plinth base of two levels, housing parking garages and a host of recreational amenities.

The entry sequence leads visitors past a pool/spa with backlit fountain into the glass/public level of the home. Breathtaking views overwhelm the senses, and sightlines across the low dining and living room are unbroken. One hundred and eighty degrees of glass, perforated intermittently by sliding glass doors enable the entire core of the home to be open to the elements, letting in both

California sunshine and the prevailing coastal breezes. Full-length, wrap-around curtains mitigate the direct sunlight when desired. The simplified manual system of operable glass doors and passive shading provides all of the temperature controls needed with minimal energy consumption.

Upstairs, private bedrooms open to a shared terrace, and the home's bottom floor, sunken into the hillside, features entertainment and recreation options, including a pool table, wine cellar with glass ceiling, screening room, weight room, and dance club, complete with DJ station, mirror ball, and full-service bar.

A light, open floor plan on every level emphasizes natural light throughout the home, and main program elements are central and low, so as not to block views to the outside. A master stair carves out the home's central volume, a shaft allowing light, sightlines, and ventilation to pass between floors.

1 Teak plywood panels float above an all-glass level in the Beuth Residence

Upstairs, living quarters offer respite from ambient sound, and provide views that touch the sky. A master suite sits directly above the living room, sharing equally magnificent 180-degree vistas through 4-foot-high windows visible from the master bed. Steps from the bedside, a sitting lounge eases the journey to wakefulness with Barcelona chairs and a window-side view for morning coffee and a glance at the morning paper. A transparent shower "partitions" the bedroom from its luxurious master bath.

A sumptuous oasis, the Beuth Residence acts at once as a home and private observatory of the busy city below—moments away from the action, a world away from its madness.

2 A galley kitchen with cross-ventilation

3 Kitchen, viewed from the dining room

2

3

4

"One hundred and eighty degrees of glass, perforated intermittently by sliding glass doors enable the entire core of the home to be open to the elements, letting in both California sunshine and the prevailing coastal breezes."

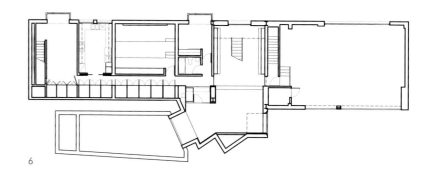

6

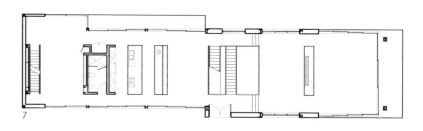

7

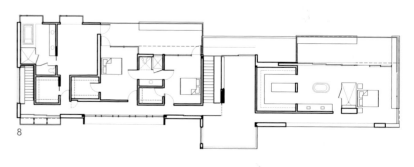

8

5

4   A sitting room just inside the main entry
5   White Barcelona chairs in a reading room
6   Level one floor plan
7   Level two, main entry level floor plan
8   Level three bedrooms floor plan

Ingjaldsdóttir Residence

Los Angeles, California
Architect: Minarch

Generous ocean breezes waft through the front door of the Ingjaldsdóttir Residence. Designed by the Icelandic architects who live inside, the home explodes with vibrant color and transparency, celebrating at once its owners' unique heritage and its communion with the near-perfect California climate.

A completely open floor plan on the main level integrates kitchen, living, and outdoor dining room into one contiguous space—encouraging social interaction. Black cabinets of child-friendly recycled tires topped with bright orange Corian hearken to the volcanoes and lava rock from the architects' home country. An Icelandic waterfall is suggested by the bright blue stairway cascading down from the second level, with a narrow wall-side water feature to reflect sunlight from above.

Entering the ground floor garden through three 8- by 8-foot sliding glass door panels, a disappearing wall welcomes the outdoor dining room into the home. The wood-floored exterior room features radiant and roof heating to accommodate cooler winter nights. An outdoor barbeque island mirrors the recycled tire/Corian combination of the kitchen cabinets.

Off the main living quarters, two bedrooms, bathrooms, and a family room are secluded from the hubbub of the main spaces. Upstairs, a Schindler-inspired master suite features a spa-like bathroom where pebbles perform reflexology on one's feet, a generous office space, and sleeping veranda to enjoy California's many warm summer nights.

Clever features of the home include a steel-framed window in the TV area surrounded by magnetic cushions that can be arranged at will, a structural H beam used as a lighting fixture, a master bed headboard that doubles as a bureau of drawers from the back, and bookshelves used as railings and visual separation between rooms.

Clad in gray concrete panels made out of 30 percent recycled paper, the exterior uses no stucco or paint. Interiors too are paint-, chemical-, carpet-, and tile-free. Permeable lava rocks surround exterior walls, allowing natural water to penetrate the soil.

1 A slatted screen adjacent to the home's entry

An oversized swivel door in the front welcomes prevailing breezes and a panel of wood louvers passively shades bedrooms on the ground floor from direct sunlight. During California's short winters, hydronic radiant heat warms the home through concrete and natural wood floors.

Cool and airy, the Ingjaldsdóttir Residence inserts a slice of Icelandic playfulness into feverishly modern California architecture—the visitor is excited by warm sunlight, a cool sea breeze, and playful, recycled materials where they are least expected.

2 Orange Corian counters atop recycled rubber cabinet facings
3 Minimal, translucent blue stairs emulate a waterfall

2

"An oversized swivel door in the front welcomes prevailing breezes and a panel of wood louvers passively shades bedrooms on the ground floor from direct sunlight."

3

4

4 Floor plans
5 Master bedroom
6 Slatted teak shower mat
7 A skylight in the master bathroom
8 A recycled rubber sink in the
   master bathroom

5

6

7

8

Index of Architects and Designers

Artwork Credits

Skyline Residence (page 84)
Acrylic with loose powder pigment furniture
Designer: Elisabeth Page Smith
www.elizabethpaigesmith.com
info@epsdesign.com

**Hybrid Residence (page 120) and Manhattan Beach
Residence (page 94)**
Paintings by Bill Lagattuta on pages 93, 95, 97,
99, 123
www.billlagattuta.com

**Hybrid Residence (page 120) and Santini Residence
(page 156)**
Paintings by Patrizia Martiradonna on pages 127,
160, 161
www.martiradonna.net

Images and concept: Claudio Santini
www.claudiosantini.com
write@claudiosantini.com

Claudio Santini portrait (back flap)
by Natalia K Photo